A–Z of
Lifelong Learning

GH00480592

www.ealing.gov.uk

91400000394793

A–Z of
Lifelong Learning

Jonathan Tummons and Ewan Ingleby

Mc Graw Hill Education Open University Press

Open University Press
McGraw-Hill Education
McGraw-Hill House
Shoppenhangers Road
Maidenhead
Berkshire
England
SL6 2QL

email: enquiries@openup.co.uk
world wide web: www.openup.co.uk

and Two Penn Plaza, New York, NY 10121-2289, USA

First published 2014

A catalogue record of this book is available from the British Library

ISBN-13: 978-0-335-26324-0
ISBN-10: 0-335-26324-0
eISBN: 978-0-335-26325-7

Library of Congress Cataloging-in-Publication Data
CIP data applied for

Typeset by Aptara Inc., India

Praise for this book

"This book is an excellent entry point for anyone who wants to know more about lifelong learning and the lifelong learning sector. Each entry provides a clear definition and an introduction to the topic with an overview of the key elements. This is followed by a concise critical review highlighting the key theorists and writers. Each section concludes with a comprehensive guide to further reading.

Jonathan Tummons and Ewan Ingleby combine scholarship and experience of the sector with the outcomes of their own research to create a valuable addition to the literature on lifelong learning.

If you are unfamiliar with the territory of lifelong learning, this book gives you the map."

Pete Scales, Senior Lecturer in Education, University of Derby, UK

"In their introduction, Tummons and Ingleby describe the breadth and complexity of the lifelong learning sector with its wide range of educational institutions, programmes of study, contexts and settings and diverse student and teacher populations. That it manages so comprehensively to encompass this sector, from 'Accreditation of Prior Learning' to 'Zone of Proximal Development', is one of the key achievements of this text. Each entry is economically written but any necessary brevity does not prevent the writers from dealing with topics in a critical and scholarly fashion and entries are usefully accompanied by references and further reading. The indices of most textbooks concerned with the sector will usually indicate where, through the text, individual topics are dealt with. A strong feature of A-Z of Lifelong Learning is that readers can go directly to topics which interest them for a clear, comprehensive treatment of them. This text will be invaluable to all those teaching or studying in the sector and will be particularly useful for those outside the sector baffled by the myriad topics, theories, policies, processes which are current within it – indeed, there is even an entry on 'Jargon'!"

Andrew Armitage, Head of the Department of Post-Compulsory Education, Canterbury Christ Church University, UK

"This is a welcome and timely text. Lifelong learning is characterised by continual revision and radical diversity. This simple A-Z of the *sector provides a much needed overview of that complexity. For the novice unfamiliar with the pedagogies, philosophies and policies that define working with adults – this A-Z of Lifelong Learning is an accessible introduction. The seasoned professional familiar with a particular institutional setting will appreciate gaining depth and insight into the workings of an entirely different educational context. Those working in a further education college may know little and understand less about the distinctiveness of the Workers' Educational Association. Each alphabetically listed entry is sharply focussed and accessibly written. The writers somehow manage to stay true to the criticality and contention desired by those seeking depth. They do more than provide factual information; the reader is gently guided through the broad arguments surrounding that particular entry – audit, Ofsted and part-time tutors are three good examples of how contestation is introduced: there is enough here to appreciate the significance of the concept but too little to completely satisfy. The reader is left curious and inspired, wanting to follow up and find out more. Yet, each entry provides just enough detail to stimulate thought and discussion."*

Carol Azumah Dennis, PCET Programme Director, University of Hull, UK

Contents

Introduction: The lifelong learning sector   1

A   9

Accreditation of prior learning   9
Action research   11
Adult learners   12
Agency   14
Andragogy   15
Assessment   16
Audit   18

B   21

Benefits of learning   21
Body language   22
Brain-based learning theory   23

C   26

Coaching   26
Communication   27
Communities of practice   29
Constructivism   30
Continuing professional development   32
Curriculum   33

D   36

Development   36
Differentiation   37
Disabilities   39
Distance learning   40
Diversity   41
Dual professionalism   42

E   45

Edutainment   45
E-learning   46
Employability   48
Empowerment   49
Experiential learning   50

F   54

Family learning   54
Flexible learning   55
Formal learning   56
Functional skills   58
Further education   59

G   61

Gender   61

H   63

Higher education   63
Human capital   64

I   67

Inclusion   67
Informal learning   68
Institute for Learning   70
IQER   71

J   73

Jargon   73

K   75

Key skills   75
Knowledge   76

L   80

Learners   80
Learning   82

Learning styles   83
Lesson planning   84
Liberal tradition   86
Lifelong learning   87

M   90

Mentees   90
Mentors   91
Mixed Economy Group, and HE in FE   92
Motivation   94

N   97

NEETS   97

O   99

Observations   99
Offender learning   100
Ofsted   101
Outreach   102

P   105

Part-time tutors   105
Pastoral care   106
Pedagogy   108
Personalised learning   110
Professional learning   111
Professionalism   113

Q   116

Qualifications   116
Quality assurance   117

R   120

Recreational learning   120
Reflective practice   122
Research   123
Resources   125

S   127

Safeguarding   127
Schemes of work   128
Self-directed learning   129
Skills   131
Social learning theory   132
Social policy   134
Syllabus   135

T   137

Teaching   137
Technology-enhanced learning   138
Theory   140
Training   141
Transformative learning   142

U   145

Underachievement   145

V   147

Values   147
Vocational education   148
Vocationalism and new vocationalism   150
Voice   151

W   154

Widening participation   154
Wolf report   155
Work-based learning   157
Workers' Educational Association   158

Y   161

Youth work   161

Z   163

Zone of proximal development   163

Index   165

Introduction: The lifelong learning sector

This book provides an A–Z of the lifelong learning sector. Ingleby and Hunt (2008) refer to the sector as being characterised by a range of educational institutions (further education colleges, adult education centres, outreach centres, family learning units, libraries, museums, and so forth) offering an even more varied range of formal and informal educational programmes. The lifelong learning sector can be a fascinating educational context to work and learn in. It is characterised by diversity and difference. There are a number of different groups of students within this educational context. There are also a number of different programmes of study. This range of contexts and learners is valued and regarded highly by many of the staff and students who are part of the lifelong learning sector. Anecdotally, many staff associated with the lifelong learning sector highlight the range of teaching experiences that they encounter within this educational context. Staff may be involved in both further and higher education, in accredited adult education, or in family learning programmes involving both parents or guardians and children. They may teach teenage learners who have only recently left school alongside adults who left school many years before. The variety of teaching experiences is one of the enduring appeals of this educational context. The settings that are used for teaching are similarly characterised by diversity. Many of the older educational institutions have their origins in the technical colleges of the late nineteenth and early twentieth centuries, and the university extension departments that grew alongside the post-war educational expansion of the 1950s and 1960s. There are also teaching centres in the community – in churches, in rooms attached to primary schools, and in community centres. The lifelong learning sector also involves education that occurs within local libraries, art galleries, and museums.

The students who are educated in the lifelong learning sector come from a range of educational backgrounds. In further education colleges, there are younger students who are studying vocational subjects such as carpentry alongside adults who are studying foundation degrees in child development. In schools, there are parents studying so that they can help their children with their homework. And in community centres, there are adult learners researching the histories of their local communities through old photographs. This diverse range of students requires a diverse range of subject specialists to meet their needs. Some tutors were until recently working in industry and have changed career to become teachers. There are other tutors who continue to work in business while teaching on a part-time basis. And there are those tutors who were themselves 'non-traditional' students in the lifelong learning sector, and others who are qualified to PhD level. There is certainly no such thing as a 'typical' teacher or trainer in the lifelong learning sector.

Tummons (2010: 23) cites 1 January 2005 as a pivotal moment in the recent development of the emerging UK lifelong learning sector. This date witnessed the establishment of LLUK (Lifelong Learning UK) under New Labour. LLUK operated as the body responsible for the professional development of all employees within the lifelong learning sector until its closure in 2011 under the Coalition government. Alongside LLUK, a subsidiary organisation called Standards Verification UK (SVUK) assumed responsibility for approving and endorsing teacher training qualifications within the post-compulsory sector (SVUK also ceased operations in March 2011 as a consequence of the Coalition government's closure of quangos in order to save costs). The responsibility for occupational standards was once that of the Further Education Teaching Organisation (FENTO), the predecessor of LLUK and SVUK. Moreover, at the same time, the Department for Education and Skills (DfES) introduced a new range of qualifications for teacher training in the post-16 sector. This culminated in the introduction of a new set of occupational standards in 2007. These new standards replaced the FENTO standards in order to emphasise the importance of the sector responding to a broad lifelong learning agenda. The DfES considered that the previous FENTO standards were limited due to their focus on 'further education'. In contrast, 'lifelong learning' was deemed to cover all aspects of post-compulsory learning. However, just as the FENTO standards were considered to be no longer fit for purpose, so the LLUK standards are now in the process of being rewritten or revised by the recently formed Education and Training Foundation, working alongside the Institute for Learning.

This brief summary of what has happened in the lifelong learning sector reveals that it is an educational context that is not static. It is characterised by changing practice, changing politics, changing standards, changing buildings, and changing learners. The process of working in the sector is based on learning, experience, and reflective practice. This book engages with the fascinating processes that characterise the lifelong learning sector by providing an A–Z outline of key aspects that define this educational context.

This book

This book identifies key factors associated with the lifelong learning sector. These key factors form the characteristics that define this educational context. One of the reasons why the lifelong learning sector is a fascinating educational arena is the many factors that continue to influence the teaching and learning that occurs within the sector. There are differing understandings of pedagogy within the sector. 'Brain-based learning theory' occurs alongside other forms of pedagogy. In recent years, there has been discussion over the application of 'learning styles' to pedagogy in the lifelong learning sector. As well as these discussions over differing forms of pedagogy, there are also debates between the types of staff employed within the sector over what the lifelong learning sector should actually represent. The rising influence of Ofsted (the Office for Standards in Education, Children's Services, and Skills) within the English lifelong learning sector has resulted in an emphasis being placed on 'audit' and 'inspection'. The 'managerialism' that coordinates the inspection process has also emerged as a central aspect of the working practices of lifelong learning. This has led to 'quality assurance' processes appearing to be as important as the teaching that occurs and the learners who are taught.

Much of the book content focuses on types of teaching and learning within the lifelong learning sector. Alongside pedagogy there is andragogy, with adult learners who can have very different needs to younger learners. The type of teaching that occurs with older learners may be based more on 'coaching', in contrast to the didactic teaching that traditionally occurred within educational settings. 'Flexible learning' may be of more benefit to these learners. The 'employability' agenda influencing the lifelong learning sector is also outlined within the book. A narrow curriculum of English, ICTs (information communication technologies), maths, and science may be taught within the lifelong learning sector. This emphasis on employability skills may be phrased formally as 'key skills' of 'functional skills'. The consequences for teaching and learning are witnessed in the 'lesson plans' and 'schemes of work' that are used by the staff teaching in the sector.

The book also outlines competing philosophies about education within the lifelong learning sector. The 'liberal tradition' with its emphasis on the freedom of the individual is contrasted with the emphasis that is placed on achieving 'qualifications'. A focus on achieving qualifications draws attention to the 'end product' of the lifelong learning sector as opposed to reflecting on the 'processes' resulting in the 'end product'. 'Self-directed learning' is contrasted with the formal 'teaching' that has always been part of the lifelong learning sector.

As the lifelong learning sector is frequently influenced by the agendas of governments, much of the content of the book outlines the consequences of government policies. There may be a limitation of 'agency' as the politicians – with their various political goals – shape the lifelong learning sector. The 'benefits of learning' may be reduced due to the influence of political agendas on the lifelong learning sector. The 'professional development' that occurs (or does not occur) within the lifelong learning sector is likely to be influenced by these political ideals. Coffield (2006) draws attention to the influence of politicians and economists within education in the UK. The establishment of an 'Institute for Learning' with its requirement for a particular number of hours of 'continuing professional development' is a consequence of the influence of politicians and economists on the lifelong learning sector. The 'jargon' that is used to describe the sector is also influenced by this economic and political agenda.

The lifelong learning sector is associated with change and variation. Much of the book's content outlines the nature of this variable practice. There are competing interpretations of knowledge within the lifelong learning sector. The 'formal learning' that occurs can appear to be in contrast to the 'experiential learning' that also occurs within the sector. The traditional learners studying at degree level within the lifelong learning sector can appear to be at odds with those students who are studying on 'NVQ' programmes. The students who are referred to as 'NEETs' can demonstrate a 'pastoral need' and this can in turn inspire new interpretations of pedagogy in the lifelong learning sector. The presence of programmes for 'offender learners' occurs alongside 'professional learning' for accountants, teachers, and local government workers. All of these 'ingredients' go towards forming this fascinating educational context.

In this way, through focusing on important concepts, moments, stakeholders, and theories, it is hoped that this book will provide the reader with an up-to-date snapshot of the sector, while at the same time providing the criticality and depth of scholarship that the study and understanding of the sector both requires and deserves.

Contemporary factors influencing teaching and learning in the lifelong learning sector

Selwyn (2011: 395) notes that those observers who predicted that the first UK hung parliament since 1974 would result in 'bland politics' have been proved wrong. In education there have emerged a series of policies (including academy schools and reform of the GCSE exam system) that are characterised by a sense of ambition (even if the policies fail to convince the general public of their merits). Moreover, this approach to policy began within the immediate term of the new Coalition administration in 2010. There has been an active reversal of the policy of the previous administration due to the perceived need for spending cuts of up to 30 per cent in departmental budgets. Alongside this move to actively reject the policy approaches of New Labour emerged the concept of a 'big society'. At the centre of this misleading term is a notion of 'small government'. The concept is based on an attempt to reduce state involvement in public services so that there is devolution of power to individual 'citizens' (remembering that the UK does not have a written constitution) alongside increased involvement of the private sector.

The political changes of May 2010 have resulted in substantial and far-reaching policy adjustments and reforms within UK education. Selwyn (2011: 396) goes on to urge academics to 'scrutinise the emerging educational intentions of the Coalition administration' by asking 'how, why and with what likely outcomes these redirections of policy are taking shape'. The current lifelong learning sector has been influenced by the policy approaches of the Coalition government. A renewed emphasis on developing the skills that are perceived to be necessary for employability has been one of these consequences for the lifelong learning sector, alongside wider curriculum change (particularly in relation to the provision and organisation of apprenticeships), reform of qualifications and examinations systems (particularly in relation to those programmes of study that were, according to the Wolf Report, not leading students to meaningful progression to further training or employment), and reform of professional qualifications for teachers and trainers across the lifelong learning sector (through the reintroduction of voluntarism in relation to teaching qualifications).

Minott (2010) and Tigelaar *et al.* (2005) are opposed to regarding 'education' and 'employability' as synonyms. These authors argue that education ought to be characterised by the consideration of existing knowledge, beliefs, and experiences in order to enable reflective practice. Minott (2010) considers the crucial goal of education to be 'reflection'. Minott (2010: 327) argues that reflecting on an 'understanding of what works' within teaching and learning informs the effective teaching which in turn enhances student learning. It can be argued that this process is more likely to occur within the lifelong learning sector if reflective practice is encouraged. This enables a new pedagogy that is not based on meeting standards and employability agendas but which encourages teachers and learners to develop the curriculum for academic reasons alone.

Minott (2010) goes on to argue that building work-related knowledge requires an attitude of inquiry. This 'self-directed professional development' realises a move of responsibility away from others towards the individual. He proposes that if this process is to occur, the organisation that the individual works in needs to support this way of thinking. If this type of pedagogy is to occur in the lifelong learning sector, there needs to be the facilitation of reflection at both the individual and organisational level. Minott (2010: 329) also suggests that this reflective process is more likely to occur when there is an examination of the prevailing work ethos:

> Teacher educators need to develop the ability to link their own teaching to theory in order to 'model' what they teach. This requires that they should not only be familiar with theories found in books and articles but must also be able to make those theories real and connect them to their practice, and that of their student teachers.

In these lines, Minott is arguing in favour of a link between teaching theory and teaching practice. The recommendation is for shared understandings of teaching and learning in order to nourish and develop the educational context.

The recommendation to not only 'talk the talk' but also to 'walk the walk' is based on a desire to combine what Urban (2008) considers as uniting 'ways of knowing' and 'ways of being'. The difficulty appears to be when these aspects of education in the lifelong learning sector become separated. One of the implications of this argument is that, ideally, there ought to be the creation of participatory dialogues that enable a shared understanding of education. This in turn is more likely to allow a bridging of the gap between policy and practice within a professional system. The consequence of such a shared vision of education in the lifelong learning sector is based on an acceptance of 'difference, diversity, and the messiness of human life rather than seeking, in the first instance, to resolve it' (Schwandt, 2004: 40).

McKeon and Harrison (2010: 26) cite the work of Loughran (2006) to define pedagogy as 'the art and science of educating focusing on the relationship between learning and teaching'. As noted previously, the presence of an employability agenda alongside the critics of this agenda reveals that there are competing understandings of pedagogy within the lifelong learning sector. Pedagogical practitioners may be encouraged to reflect upon the importance of what McKeon and Harrison (2010: 26) refer to as the 'what, the how and the why' of teaching. Developing pedagogical skills links to what Hamilton *et al.* (2009) describe as 'what' is being taught and 'how' it is being taught during teaching sessions. The consequence is that an emphasis is placed on pedagogical reasoning within the formal academic curriculum. This notion of uniting 'what' is being taught with 'how' content is taught offers a potential resolution of the standards-driven employability agenda that Lucas (2007) defines as looking purely at 'what is taught'.

It can be argued that there are benefits to emphasising the importance of developing professional identity in the lifelong learning sector. McKeon and Harrison (2010: 27) refer to professional identity as a 'socially and culturally constructed self, formed through life's experiences'. The notion of 'professional identity' acknowledges that the process of developing professional skills is not static but based on what McKeon and Harrison (2010: 27), MacLure (1993) and – originally – Lave and Wenger (1991) phrase as participating in 'communities of practice'. Professional identity may be understood in relation to others and their professional roles. McKeon and Harrison (2010: 27) amplify this understanding of professional identity by referring to Wenger's (1998: 55) idea that professionalism, as an aspect of an individual's identity, incorporates 'the past and the future in the very process of negotiating the present'. The essence of this idea is that those individuals involved in teaching form a productive community of practice that can be used to enhance professional activity. The knowledge, experiences, and stories of tutors with differing levels of expertise can be used to grow a shared professional identity, which in turn can be used to develop pedagogical practice. However, such conversations and reflections do require time and space – commodities that are increasingly scarce in a lifelong learning sector that is driven by managerialism and audit.

McKeon and Harrison (2010: 28) argue that pedagogy involves the 'formation and transformation of identity as experiences are interpreted and reinterpreted'. This is essentially similar to the kind of reflective practice that is recommended by Minott. For Minott (2010: 326), self-directed professional development is considered as referring to the building up of work-related knowledge in order to enhance professional performance. Professional and personal development is regarded as being linked together. The challenge in achieving self-directed reflective practice is revealed by McKeon and Harrison (2010: 28), who apply the work of Coldron and Smith (1999) to argue that professional identity is neither 'isolated' nor 'totally personal'. The process occurs 'within the socially and culturally constructed context of the world of education'. This awareness of factors influencing the lifelong learning sector has helped to establish the content of the book. The emphasis placed on meeting the requirements of audit alongside an employability agenda influences our understanding of the lifelong learning sector. This links to the arguments of Coffield *et al.* (2004), Downie and Randall (1999), Lieberman (2009), and Urban (2008). In other words, education that develops individuals is essentially contrasted to standards-driven (or bureaucratic) education. This is the paradox that lies at the heart of any critical reading of the lifelong learning sector and which, it is hoped, this book will help to critique and explore.

References and further reading

Coffield, F. (2006) *Running ever faster down the wrong road*. Inaugural Lecture, University of London Institute of Education, London.

Coffield, F., Moseley, D., Hall, E. and Ecclestone, K. (2004) *Learning Styles and Pedagogy in Post-16 Learning: A Systematic and Critical Review*. London: LSDA.

Coldron, J. and Smith, R. (1999) Active location in teachers' construction of their professional identities, *Journal of Curriculum Studies*, 31(1), 711–26.

Downie, R. and Randall, F. (1999) *Palliative Care Ethics: A Companion for All Specialities*. Oxford: Oxford University Press.

Hamilton, M., Loughran, J. and Marcondes, M. (2009) Teacher educators and the self-study of teaching practices, in A. Swennen and M. Van der Klink (eds.) *Becoming a Teacher Educator: Theory and Practice for Teacher Educators*. Dordrecht: Springer.

Ingleby, E. and Hunt, J. (2008) The CPD needs of mentors in post-compulsory initial teacher training in England, *Journal of In-Service Education*, 34(1), 61–75.

Lave, J. and Wenger, E. (1991) *Situated Learning: Legitimate Peripheral Participation*. Cambridge: Cambridge University Press.

Lieberman, J. (2009) Reinventing teacher professional norms and identities: the role of lesson study and learning communities, *Professional Development in Education*, 35(1), 83–99.

Loughran, J. (2006) *Developing Pedagogy of Teacher Education*. London: Routledge.

Lucas, N. (2007) The in-service training of adult literacy, numeracy and English for Speakers of Other Languages teachers in England: the challenges of a 'standards-led model', *Journal of In-Service Education*, 33(1), 125–42.

MacLure, M. (1993) Arguing for your self: identity as an organising principle in teachers' jobs and lives, *British Educational Research Journal*, 19(4), 311–22.

McKeon, F. and Harrison, J. (2010) Developing pedagogical practice and professional identities of beginning teacher educators, *Professional Development in Education*, 36(1), 25–44.

Minott, M.A. (2010) Reflective teaching as self-directed professional development: building practical or work-related knowledge, *Professional Development in Education*, 36(1), 325–38.

Schwandt, T.A. (2004) Hermeneutics: a poetics of inquiry versus a methodology for research, in H. Piper and I. Stronach (eds.) *Educational Research: Difference and Diversity*. Aldershot: Ashgate.

Selwyn, N. (2011) The place of technology in the Conservative-Liberal Democrat education agenda: an ambition of absence?, *Educational Review*, 63(4), 395–408.

Tigelaar, D., Dolmanns, D., Grave, W., Wolfhangen, I. and Vleuten, C. (2005) Participants' opinions on the usefulness of a teaching portfolio, *Medical Education*, 40(4), 371–8.

Tummons, J. (2010) *Becoming a Professional Tutor in the Lifelong Learning Sector* (2nd edn.). Exeter: Learning Matters.

Urban, M. (2008) Dealing with uncertainty: challenges and possibilities for the early childhood profession, *European Early Childhood Education Research Journal*, 16(2), 135–52.

Wenger, E. (1998) *Communities of Practice: Learning, Meaning and Identity*. New York: Cambridge University Press.

Winnicott, D.W. (1987) *The Child, the Family and the Outside World*. Cambridge: Perseus Press.

A

Accreditation of prior learning
Action research
Adult learners
Agency
Andragogy
Assessment
Audit

Accreditation of prior learning

The accreditation of prior learning (APL) is a process by which a student's previous learning (whether *formal learning* or *informal learning*) can be formally recognised and certificated by an educational institution. That is, it is a process that provides students with the opportunity to receive recognition for learning that has resulted from prior work and life experience, or from past attendance at a further education college or adult education centre, and allows institutions to recognise and give credit for this learning. The accreditation of prior learning is used within institutions in two main ways.

First, it can be used as a process that allows applicants who lack the required formal qualifications or other prerequisites to gain entry to further and adult education courses. This makes APL an important part of the drive to widen access to education for people who in the past have been underrepresented in education and training such as particular social or ethnic groups. It also makes it easier for people with no formal qualifications to re-enter education. It opens up all kinds of education, training, and accreditation opportunity for people who lack formal qualifications and certificates but can still prove that 'they can do it' – that they have achieved a particular skill, competence or understanding. Such diverse learning from experience is just as important as the learning that takes place in schools and colleges, and

APL provides a method by which it can be recognised and perhaps rewarded, thereby motivating people to re-enter formal education when they might otherwise have been excluded.

Second, the accreditation of prior learning can be used as a process that allows students who are currently enrolled on a programme of study to gain exemption from one or more components or modules within the programme. This is usually because the modules in question are very closely aligned to a course or module that the student has previously undertaken at a different institution, but it is also possible for informal learning to be accredited in this way. Thus APL provides a way for students to 'top-up' prior programmes of study, or to return to study after a period away (for example, due to changes in employment or family circumstances).

APL refers to prior learning that has been accredited and where a certificate, or other formal record of achievement, has been awarded on successful completion. In such circumstances, it is a straightforward process for an institution to evaluate the certificates or other formal records of achievement, such as module transcripts, that a student or applicant might choose to present. For students and applicants who wish to gain credit for informal learning, a slightly different process is used – the accreditation of prior experiential learning (APEL). This usually requires the student to compile a portfolio of evidence that can demonstrate that they have already met the requirements of the course or module that they are seeking exemption from, and would typically involve:

- evidence of achievement in the workplace, such as letters of commendation or documents demonstrating workplace responsibilities;
- documents or objects/materials demonstrating achievement in the workplace, possibly created by the student at work;
- reports from references or testimonials written by employers, clients or customers;
- evidence drawn from community or voluntary activities.

APL/APEL thus forms an important element of the widening participation agenda, but it is not without its critics. Although the APL process is relatively straightforward, the disputable nature of experiential learning – of how such informal learning can or should be reclassified according to the requirements of a written curriculum – renders APEL more problematic. And while some students who have been allowed onto a course have achieved success, some of these have only done so through the provision of considerable additional support; and others have been 'set up to fail' by a process that has allowed them access to a curriculum that they were not fully prepared for.

Action research

Bryman (2004) and McNiff and Whitehead (2005) note that action research, defined as a type of research in which the researcher is responsible for changing processes, is a popular research model within the lifelong learning sector. Research participants are invited to engage at various stages of a relatively fast-moving research process involving research-action-research-action. The research process can be used to investigate professional practice in order to propose solutions to professional challenges. The process can be extended indefinitely as the original focus of concern moves to other areas.

Action research is associated with the work of Kurt Lewin (1890–1947). Lewin's action research cycle is a cycle of planning, action, and fact finding about the result of the action. Lewin's process of change involves three key components:

1. The research cycle begins with a series of planning actions by the researcher(s) and the research participants. The main elements of the research process at this stage of the research include a preliminary diagnosis, the gathering of data, feedback of results, and cooperative action planning.
2. The second stage of the action research cycle is the action or transformative stage. This stage includes actions that relate to learning processes and to planning changes in the organisation being researched. Following reflection, these actions are implemented as part of the transformation stage.
3. The third stage of the process is the production of results from the research process. This stage includes changes in behaviour resulting in corrective actions following the second stage. Reflections on data gathering are used to refine the research process.

The value of action research in terms of producing a valuable model of research for the lifelong learning sector is obvious. As opposed to having a linear research model where a hypothesis is proposed and the hypothesis is proved or disproved, a cyclical research model is in operation. However, a number of criticisms have been levelled at the application of the action research model:

1. The cyclical nature of the research process can mean that it can become difficult to fully implement the action research cycle. Students doing research in the lifelong learning sector may opt to choose action research as their model of research and then find that they are unable to complete the research cycle in its entirety. This may mean

that it is better to adopt a small-scale focus by applying a more manageable interactive model of research.

2. Linked to this criticism is the argument that the action research cycle could go on indefinitely. This could lead to a conflict within the current ethos of the lifelong learning sector with its wish to quantify teaching and learning. A cyclical model that can be ever cyclical may appear to be at odds with the wish to have results than can measure educational performance in a definitive way.

3. Action research may be characterised by bias. This is because the researcher is not detached from the research participants. In professional research on teaching, the researcher is often a teacher doing research on teaching and learning. This can mean that it is difficult to have a sense of detachment from the area of research.

At even an anecdotal level the practicalities with action research as a research model become apparent. When does research stop and action begin? When do research participants become colleagues working together to produce excellent professional practice? Are research participants and professional colleagues the same? In view of the complexities of the action research process, it is surprising that those researching the lifelong learning sector so often use action research as a research model.

Adult learners

Changing political and educational trends have led to a proliferation of terms to describe those students in formal education or training who are adults, including 'adult learners', 'mature students', and 'adult returners'. Clearly, it is difficult to find a single term for such a diffuse group of students. Adult learning theories refer to the adult learner as distinct from the child learner, but with little agreement over when this state of adulthood is reached. Self-advocacy movements (which have a strong tradition in the adult education sector) assume that any adult who is in either part-time or full-time education, and who wishes to refer to himself or herself as a mature student, is one.

There are many theoretical models that relate to adult learning (*andragogy* is one of the best known), and the ways in which adult learners are accommodated within further education colleges and adult education sectors are more or less directly influenced by such theories. For example, the *motivation* of mature students is often assumed not to be a problem compared with that of 14- to 16-year-old students within a college. In fact, such a stereotypical approach is mistaken. There are also longer standing approaches to working with adult learners that have been influential in forming attitudes around the practice of adult learning and assessment (Rogers, 2001; Rogers, 2002):

1. Problem-based learning and teaching activities are well suited to adult learners, who are able to direct their own learning. Such approaches also help mark out the adult education classroom as being qualitatively different from that of the school.
2. Adult learners may lack confidence if they have been away from formal education and training for some time. The learning and teaching strategies chosen should reflect this, and should be structured in such a way that the student can benefit from more formal instruction that can be gradually withdrawn as they progress through their chosen programme of study.
3. Adult learners' histories can have a considerable impact on their learning. This can be in terms of prior personal experiences of education (typically formed during school years) or in terms of peer or family attitudes towards education.
4. Adult learners choose to take up a course of study or training for all sorts of reasons that might not be directly concerned with the actual subject or topic being taught. Research into the wider benefits of adult learning has demonstrated the important role that adult education can play in sustaining social contact and self-esteem and contributing to mental health.
5. Barriers to participation by adult learners are often connected to the day-to-day requirements of their lives, such as the need to arrange childcare, difficulties in accessing transport, and balancing work and family commitments with attending classes and completing private study tasks.

Assessment is a particularly complex issue for both adult learners and adult educators. For many years, the influence of the *liberal tradition* of adult education could be felt in the reluctance of many adult educators to impose formal assessment regimes on their students. Similarly, assessment is often cited as a significant barrier to participation among adults who are considering a return to learning, often reflecting negative attitudes to formal education that were formed during school years – the requirements to sit formal examinations can be particularly fraught. Changes since the mid-1990s to the ways in which adult education was funded saw the gradual imposition of assessment onto adult learning programmes as a condition of maintaining funding, leading to a decline in provision and although voluntary associations such as the University of the Third Age (which provides opportunities for learners who wish to take part in learning for entirely recreational reasons) continue to thrive, participation rates have continued to decline.

Agency

Agency is a term that is often associated with the work of the German social scientist Max Weber (1864–1920). Agency refers to the actions of individuals. Weberian theory may be considered as an appealing lens through which to view the lifelong learning sector. The notion of *verstehen*, with its implication that the individual should be the primary unit of analysis, helps us to understand the changing context of the lifelong learning sector. *Verstehen* also links to debates within education about natural and social sciences and whether the methodology of the former can be applied to the latter (Weber, 1968: 4–24). Statements like 'our world-class science and research base is inherently valuable' (Department for Business, Innovation and Skills, 2010: 3) in 'The Allocation of Science and Research Funding 2011/12 to 2014/15' draw attention to the importance of funding scientific research in education. This funding priority is often made at the expense of other forms of education funding that are viewed as being less important. Weber focused on the individual human agents that led to this situation.

Whitehead (2010: 6) argues that Weber's concept of *verstehen* can be combined with his analysis of bureaucracy to give a powerful insight into the mechanics of how individual human agents shape UK policy. Weber (1968) explains that the word 'bureaucracy' has its origins in the eighteenth century and means 'rule by officials within organisations'. The argument is advanced that bureaucracy is the most efficient form of organisation, since it is exemplified by precision, continuity, discipline, strictness, and reliability. Allbrow (1970: 47) notes that one of Weber's concerns was that bureaucracy would become so large that it 'controlled the policy and action of the organisation it was supposed to serve'. Weber (1968) outlines an ideal type of bureaucracy that can be summarised as having a specialised division of labour where different individuals become responsible for specialised tasks in pursuit of organisational goals. Weber developed the view that a major feature of modern capitalist societies is the trend towards rationalisation. This conveys an emphasis on what Whitehead (2010: 6) refers to as 'planned, technical, calculable and efficient processes' that are devoid of emotion. A situation emerges in which bureaucracy becomes regarded as being the most technically efficient form of domination in modern capitalist societies, but personalism pays a heavy price. Whitehead (2010) outlines how a loss of personalism in the US higher education system has led to the emergence of a Weberian rationalism as academics are encouraged to be 'entrepreneurs'. Once more, it is individual human agents who have generated this social situation.

The work of Weber can be applied to understand the changing dynamics of education in the lifelong learning sector. Weber draws attention to the inventiveness of individual human agents as they engage with educational processes. Moreover, this notion of inventive individuals helps us to understand why much of the lifelong learning sector is in a state of flux. Weber argues that the power of individuals is such that they are able to engage with social structures to reinvent fresh understandings of the social world. This argument opposes the view that external social structures are most important in shaping the human world. The argument can be linked to the philosophy of Immanuel Kant and his emphasis on how individuals engage with the phenomena they experience in their social worlds. Some authors (e.g. Ingleby and Tummons, 2012) have engaged with this idea in their discussion of mentoring in the lifelong learning sector. In many debates, it is difficult to accept one side of the argument at the expense of the other. In the debate over 'structure' and 'agency', it makes sense to accept that both elements are important.

Andragogy

Andragogy, defined variously as a 'theory of adult learning' or 'the art and science of adult learning', is a term popularised by Malcolm Knowles (1913–1997). In its most widely recognised form, as laid out by Knowles, andragogy offers a series of six key assumptions (initially four, but Knowles refined his approach over the course of several publications) regarding adult learning and adult learners, which in turn can be seen as resting on humanistic approaches to learning, and which are proposed in direct contrast to pedagogy, which Knowles – and his followers – defined in terms of the teaching and learning of children. The six key components of Knowles' approach are:

1. Adults need to know *why* they need to learn something before the learning process can begin.
2. Because adults are responsible for their own lives, this self-concept of autonomy is extended to learning. As such, adults show a preference for *self-directed learning*.
3. Adults come to learning and education with a wealth of life experience which can – and should – form a basis or foundation for their future learning.
4. For adults to learn, the *relevance* of what is being learned needs to be clear and unambiguous. The motivation of adult learners rests on the real-world application of what is being learned.
5. Adult learners are more engaged with learning that is centred around problem-solving rather than around bodies of knowledge or content.
6. Adults are motivated to learn more by intrinsic rather than extrinsic factors.

The value of Knowles' work – as well as that of other related theorists such as Stephen Brookfield and Jack Mezirow – in terms of promoting a broader debate concerning the learning of adults, as distinct from children, is obvious. Over time, however, several factors have combined to pose a serious challenge to andragogy as a discrete framework. The problems with Knowles' theory – and with andragogy more generally – can be summarised as follows:

1. Knowles' work is based on assumptions, not empirical research. Knowles did not engage in any serious educational research in formulating his conception of andragogy, which rests predominantly on a philosophical rather than empirical position.
2. Andragogy is not a theory. The lack of any systematic inquiry based on empirical research prevents andragogy from being taken seriously as a theory. At best, it represents a framework or, arguably, an ideology, concerning the ways in which adults ought to be taught.
3. Claims regarding andragogy rest on an inadequate understanding of pedagogy. The positioning by Knowles of andragogy in 'opposition' to pedagogy rests on a narrow, and arguably incorrect, understanding of pedagogy that does not take into account contemporaneous constructivist and social constructivist approaches to the learning of children.

Indeed, even at an anecdotal level the problems with andragogy as a concept quickly emerge. When does a learner stop being a child and start being an adult? How should contemporary practitioners in the lifelong learning sector define 14- to 16-year-old learners in further education colleges – as children or as adults? Are all adult learners 'the same', equally capable of self-directed learning that rests on their own experience? In the light of these theoretical and practical critiques, perhaps the most surprising thing about andragogy is that the model continues to appear in teacher training textbooks for the lifelong learning sector, even when there is so much that is obviously wrong with it.

Assessment

Assessment is a word that, like many others in the English language, can have several meanings. Within the context of education and training, it equates to testing: if a student is being assessed, then he or she is being tested. We can identify a number of distinct types of assessment according to the stage at which they tend to occur and the purposes for which they are practised:

- *Diagnostic assessment* involves providing advice and guidance to course applicants, checking prior qualifications, and establishing the extent to which the applicant demonstrates an aptitude towards – as well as an understanding of – the programme of study. Other diagnostic assessments range from the assessment of learning styles or functional skills to the assessment of special educational needs.

- *Ipsative assessment* is an individual process, which allows the student to complete two main tasks. The first task involves the identification of the student's own prior knowledge, experience, and qualifications, allowing the student to consider and then identify any specific areas that require development or particular attention. The second task requires setting targets against which future progress can be assessed. A portfolio or individual learning plan (ILP) is often used to capture this process.

- *Formative* assessment is the assessment that takes place during a course, as a part of the learning process, and as such it is down to the teacher or trainer to design and implement it. It seeks to encourage and facilitate learning, as well as acting as a tool for the tutor, who can thereby ascertain how much learning has already taken place.

- *Summative* assessment is normally carried out at the end of a module or course. It is always a formal process, to determine whether students have acquired the skills, knowledge, behaviour or understanding that the course set out to provide them with. Summative assessment can be used to record achievement through the award of *qualifications* and to anticipate future achievement. Certification is also required to allow students to progress to higher study, or to enter the workplace.

- *Peer assessment* has seen a significant growth in recent years. It is understood as the practice of involving the entire student group in assessment. This typically involves students marking or reviewing each other's work, using time in class to discuss the course criteria that they are being assessed against. In this way, students are able to build a better understanding of the assessment process and thereby improve their performance.

Assessment practices within the post-compulsory and lifelong learning sector are distinct from those found in compulsory education in several ways. For example, there is less of a focus on traditional examinations, and a greater use of simulation and portfolio-based methods. The assessment of practical tasks is of obvious importance, as is the need to provide work-based or work-related environments for such assessments to be held in, with obvious implications for resources. And a range of staff, including assessors, verifiers, and employers – as well as college lecturers – are involved in the process.

Assessment is hotly debated among researchers and policy makers. Debates around the frequency of assessment, grade inflation, the value of formal qualifications compared with real-life experience, the extent to which assessment requirements distort curricula, the use of assessment results to rank institutions – and students! – and the extent to which assessment systems do actually measure what they intend to measure, all combine to make assessment a controversial topic. Researchers have also foregrounded the ways in which assessment systems advantage students from some socio-economic backgrounds and disadvantage others, and it can be argued that claims to the fairness of assessment systems fail to acknowledge the iniquities that are inherent within them.

Audit

Audit refers to the measurement of educational performance. An emphasis is placed upon the importance of inspection regimes and the statistics that outline who has achieved (and who has not achieved). Audit is associated with Ofsted (the Office for Standards in Education, Children's Services, and Skills). The role of Ofsted in inspecting the lifelong learning sector appears to have increased in importance over the lifetime of the last two governments in England. It can be argued that there are benefits as well as disadvantages in emphasising the importance of audit.

On the one hand, unregulated educational processes cannot be assessed in a thorough way. It is difficult to know what is of benefit to all learners and all teachers if there is no process of audit. Education becomes deregulated. It is impossible to assess the performance of education in the UK. Moreover, it is difficult to identify international standards of education in the absence of a process of audit. On the other hand, too much audit can lead to an emphasis being placed upon the 'product' as opposed to the 'process' (Urban, 2008). The conflation of the inspection processes can also result in too much emphasis being placed on the end product. To apply an analogy, weighing the animal does not increase the weight of the animal. Similarly, inspecting the educational process does not necessarily improve that educational process.

The work of a number of authors draws attention to the oppressive nature of a culture of audit that appears within the lifelong learning sector (Freire, 1973, 1985, 1994; Torres, 1998, 2008; Giroux, 2000; Archer and Leathwood, 2003; Harris and Islar, 2013; Mayo, 2013; Morley and Dunstan, 2013; Williams, 2013). If the ideas of these authors are developed, we can criticise the audit process on moral grounds. A main objection of these authors is that current educational practices within neoliberal governments in the UK evidence oppression and exploitation (or 'unfairness'). Authors including Freire (1973, 1985, 1994), Giroux (2000), and Torres (1998) have attempted to place 'moral education' at the centre of educational policies. In contrast, the varying approaches to policy adopted by the politicians are influenced by their political beliefs and economic priorities. The perceived importance of globalisation and the need to compete with other emerging economies has been identified as a key element of teaching and learning. Assessing educational performance becomes a means of identifying how the UK is doing in international education tables. Critical pedagogy disputes the rationale behind this approach to teaching for moral reasons. Critical pedagogy is opposed to the bilateral priorities of economics and politics we see within the process of audit. There is instead a recommendation for systematic enquiries into teaching and learning in order to develop pedagogy. It is this attempt to create understandings as well as change that is at the heart of critical pedagogy. A merit of critical pedagogy is that attention is drawn to the oppressive nature of audit. Education is about realising individual potential in the fullest sense of the word. Urban (2008) argues that English education has become like the film 'The Wizard of Oz'. Instead of focusing on the 'journey', emphasis is placed on the final destination. Instead of reflecting on educational processes within the lifelong learning sector, emphasis is placed on the qualifications that are obtained. It can be argued that this focus is a product of a culture of audit.

References and further reading

Allbrow, M. (1970) *Bureaucracy*. London: Macmillan.

Archer, L. and Leathwood, C. (2003) Identities and inequalities in higher education, in L. Archer, M. Hutchings and A. Ross (eds.) *Higher Education and Social Class: Issues of Eexclusion and Inclusion*. London: Routledge Falmer.

Bryman, A. (2004) *Social Research Methods*. Oxford: Oxford University Press.

Challis, M. (1993) *Introducing APEL*. London: Routledge.

Davenport, J. (1993) Is there any way out of the andragogy morass?, in M. Thorpe, R. Edwards and A. Hanson (eds.) *Culture and Processes of Adult Learning*. London: Routledge.

Department for Business, Innovation and Skills (BIS) (2010) *The Allocation of Science and Research Funding 2011/12 to 2014/15: Investing in World-class Science and Research*. London: BIS.

Ecclestone, K. (2010) *Transforming Formative Assessment in Lifelong Learning*. Maidenhead: McGraw-Hill.

Freire, P. (1973) *Education for Critical Consciousness*. New York: Seabury Press.

Freire, P. (1985) *The Politics of Education: Culture, Power and Liberation*. South Hadley, MA: Bergin & Garvey.

Freire, P. (1994) *Pedagogy of Hope: Reliving the Pedagogy of the Oppressed*. New York: Continuum.

Friedman, M. and Friedman, R.D. (1980) *Free to Choose*. London: Penguin.

Giroux, H. (2000) *Impure Acts*. London: Taylor & Francis.

Harris, L. and Islar, M. (2013) Neoliberalism, nature and changing modalities of environmental governance in contemporary Turkey, in Y. Atasoy (ed.) *Global Economic Crisis and the Politics of Diversity*. London: Palgrave Macmillan.

Ingleby, E. and Tummons, J. (2012) Repositioning professionalism: teachers, mentors, policy and praxis, *Research in Post-Compulsory Education*, 17(2), 163–79.

Jarvis, P. (2010) *Adult Education and Lifelong Learning: Theory and Practice* (4th edn.). London: Routledge.

Mayo, P. (2013) *Echoes from Freire for a Critically Engaged Pedagogy.* London: Bloomsbury.

McNiff, J. and J. Whitehead (2005) *All You Need to Know about Action Research.* London: Sage.

Morley, C. and Dunstan, J. (2013) A response to neoliberal challenges to field education, *Social Work Education*, 32(2), 141–56.

Rogers, A. (2002) *Teaching Adults.* Buckingham: Open University Press.

Rogers, J. (2001) *Adults Learning.* Buckingham: Open University Press.

Torres, C.A. (1998) *Democracy, Education and Multiculturalism.* Lanham, MD: Rowman & Littlefield.

Torres, C.A. (2008) *Education and Neoliberal Globalisation.* New York: Taylor & Francis.

Tummons, J. (2011) *Assessing Learning in the Lifelong Learning Sector* (3rd edn.). Exeter: Sage/Learning Matters.

Urban, M. (2008) Dealing with uncertainty: challenges and possibilities for the early childhood profession, *European Early Childhood Education Research Journal*, 16(2), 135–52.

Weber, M. (1968) *Economy and Society: An Outline of Interpretive Sociology.* New York: Bedminster Press.

Whitehead, P. (2010) Social theory and probation: exploring organisational complexity within a modernising context, *Social and Public Policy Review*, 4(2), 15–33.

Williams, J. (2013) *Consuming Higher Education: Why Learning can't be Bought.* London: Bloomsbury.

B

Benefits of learning
Body language
Brain-based learning theory

Benefits of learning

The benefits of learning, beyond the impact of learning the actual body of skills or subject matter that any particular *syllabus* might contain, have been extensively researched in relation to students in the lifelong learning sector. Such research is helpful to practitioners, as it serves to move discussions about education and training away from very functional conversations that fixate on employability and the 'practical application' of what has been learned, towards the wider cultural, social, and environmental benefits that participation in formal and informal learning can provide. This is not to deny the importance of participation in formal education and training as a route to stable employment (with all that this implies for personal, familial, and social structures). But the increased emphasis on the outputs of education and training as being aligned to the world of work has served to take attention away from the other beneficial outcomes that can accrue from participation in learning.

Research carried out during the last ten years or so by staff at the Centre for Research on the Wider Benefits of Learning has proposed a number of benefits of learning beyond the immediate goals of qualifications and employment (Preston and Hammond, 2003; Feinstein et al., 2008), including:

- Adult education can increase civic participation, and increase the likelihood of voting in local and national elections.
- Further education can increase self-esteem – with consequent benefits for mental health – and facilitate social networking.
- People with better qualifications are more likely to have a healthy lifestyle, with benefits for both them and their children (if they have any). They are less likely to smoke and less likely to commit crimes.

- Adult education can increase people's social networks and work to prevent social isolation, with consequent benefits for both physical and mental health.
- Further education can increase participation in community-based activities, and promote citizenship.
- Further education colleges can act as catalysts for local and regional civic pride.

The Labour government (1997–2010) promoted an expansion in education from a wider political and philosophical perspective. Drawing on notions of social justice, Labour education policy (in part) centred on the theory that particular social as well as economic problems might be alleviated through increased participation in education and training – a perspective that to some extent would seem to be borne out by the research findings outlined above. However, a more critical perspective offered by recent research into the social benefits of learning for individuals across Europe as a whole indicates that benefits such as increased civic participation are more likely to be found in local contexts where such participation is already seen as a benefit and encouraged accordingly (Sabates *et al.*, 2012).

Body language

Gross (2010) explains that body language is an example of non-linguistic communication, in that individuals provide an indication of what they are thinking as a result of their physical behaviour. Examples of body language include facial expressions, gestures and posture. A key component of body language is that it is predominantly subconscious behaviour. If, for example, we make a sign, this is different to body language because signs are conscious expressions of communication. Body language is of interest to educationalists in determining whether learning processes are successful by reflecting on the non-verbal responses of learners. Body language is associated with psychology (for example, the behaviourist, cognitive, humanist, and psychodynamic schools of psychology). These schools of psychology are interested in body language for particular reasons:

1. Behaviourist psychologists, including Pavlov and Skinner, assess how the environment influences thought processes. Behaviourist educationalists consider how the physical environment influences learning in the lifelong learning sector and how the body language of the learners expresses these feelings.
2. Cognitive psychologists, including Piaget and Vygotsky, are interested in how environmental stimuli are processed in the brain in

order to produce reactions. Cognitive educationalists reflect on how learning tasks inform learning in the lifelong learning sector and how the body language of the learners expresses these feelings.

3. Humanist psychologists, including Rogers and Maslow, study how individuals interpret the environment according to their own unique personalities. Humanist educationalists discuss how individuals interpret the learning process in the lifelong learning sector in a unique way and how body language communicates these feelings.

4. Psychodynamic psychologists, including Freud and Erikson, investigate the relationship between conscious and unconscious thoughts. Psychodynamic educationalists consider how individuals interpret learning processes in the lifelong learning sector at conscious and subconscious levels and how body language communicates these feelings.

The inspection regimes in the lifelong learning sector (Ofsted) have drawn attention to the importance of body language by using the body language of learners as a criterion for grading lessons. Learners are expected to engage with the teaching session. If learners appear to be distracted and express this distraction through their body language, this will in turn influence the grade given for the lesson. An anecdotal example led to a grade of 'satisfactory' being given for a teaching session because one of the students was 'twirling' her hair round a finger when the lecturer was delivering didactic content. The inspector interpreted this body language as being a sign that the student was not engaging fully with the content in the session. Criticisms of body language are based on the accusation that body language is a pseudoscience. Just because a student is twirling her hair round her finger, does this mean that learning is not taking place? This criticism is similar to the criticisms levelled at Freud's psychoanalytical analysis. Subconscious actions are mysterious and have an inaccessible quality. The act of smoking a cigar may simply represent the fact that the individual so engaged likes smoking cigars. It is not necessarily a sign of anything else. Similarly, who is to say (definitively) that twirling hair round a finger is proof that a learner is not engaging with the learning process? At this anecdotal level, the practicalities of using body language to inform teaching and learning become apparent. Moreover, as Malim and Birch (1998) note, body language varies according to culture. There is no universal interpretation of body language. This makes an attempt to quantify body language in a scientific way even more challenging.

Brain-based learning theory

According to Gross (2010), brain-based learning theory assumes that thought processes are the essential factor influencing human behaviour. An important component of brain-based learning is the Gestalt theory of perception, which explore how the brain imposes patterns on the perceived world. These Gestalt theories of perception are often associated with problem-solving learning. Cognitive theory is also influenced by the developmental psychology of Piaget through focusing on the maturational factors that influence human understanding. Broadly speaking, cognitive theory is concerned with how people understand the world around them and their aptitude and capacity to learn. Cognitive theory is also concerned with learning styles and it is the fundamental basis of the educational approach known as *constructivism*. This aspect of education emphasises the role of the learner in constructing his or her own ideas and the factors that influence this process.

The 'memory' is a very complex human function that is of great interest to cognitive theorists. Memory is also of central importance to learning. Indeed, learning depends upon the memory, with the process of 'memorising' being part of one of the lowest levels of rote learning. Memorising begins with a sensory buffer. Part of the information being memorised stays in the brain for about one-fifteenth of a second, while the brain assembles it to 'make sense'. Most of us will have experienced the illusion by which a succession of still pictures presented rapidly enough appears to be moving, as it is the basis of all cinematography. Once the frame rate drops below about 16 frames per second, however, we may well become conscious of the flicker or jumps from one still image to another. Similarly, we do not hear a succession of speech sounds, but complete words or phrases. It is as if the brain waits to assemble a meaningful sound before passing it on to the next stage, which is short-term memory (STM). The human STM appears to deal best with sounds rather than visual stimuli, but this may be because visual stimuli are taken in all at once, whereas sounds are processed in a linear fashion – over time. In fact, the STM is able to hold material for about 15–30 seconds, although this can be expanded by practice. This is much shorter than we may initially realise. In general, the human memory has a capacity to memorise in the region of seven items (plus or minus two). 'Items' are defined by meaning rather than size, so it may be difficult to remember telephone numbers of more than seven digits, but if '01234' is remembered as the 'dialling code' it becomes just one item, and remembering the subsequent numbers '793156' becomes simpler. If this sequence of numbers is in turn 'chunked' (or 'associated') as being 'my work phone number', it becomes even easier to remember. This of course assumes that a label for the 'chunk' already exists in long-term memory. Theoretically, long-term memory (LTM) has infinite capacity and lasts for the rest of your life. Tulving (1985) usefully distinguishes between three components of LTM:

- *semantic memory* stores concepts and ideas;
- *episodic memory* (sometimes referred to as 'autobiographical' or narrative' memory) contains memories of events;

- *procedural memory* concerns skills and 'know-how' rather than 'know-that' knowledge.

Memory involves storing and retrieving data. We can't remember everything, which can often be frustrating (for example, 'where did I put that lesson plan that worked so well last year?'). This is because it is impossible to deal with all the information we receive. Thus efficient memory relies on forgetting lots of unimportant information, while remembering key facts. As memory is linked to learning, it is affected by the following:

- *Practice* – the more times a piece of information is encountered, the more likely it will be committed to long-term memory.
- *Stage theory* – information passes through short-term memory on its way to long-term memory.
- *Primacy* – the first thing in a list is remembered well.
- *Recency/retention* – the last thing encountered is remembered well.

References and further reading

Feinstein, L., Budge, D., Vorhaus, J. and Duckworth, K. (eds.) (2008) *The Social and Personal Benefits of Learning.* London: Institute of Education.

Gross, R. (2010) *Psychology: The Study of Mind and Behaviour.* London: Hodder & Stoughton.

Malim, T. and Birch, A. 1998. *Introductory Psychology.* London: Hodder & Stoughton.

Preston, J. and Hammond, C. (2003) Practitioner views on the wider benefits of further education, *Journal of Further and Higher Education,* 27(2), 211–22.

Sabates, R., Salter, E. and Obolenskaya, P. (2012) The social benefits of initial vocational education and training for individuals in Europe, *Journal of Vocational Education and Training,* 64(3), 233–44.

Tulving, E. (1985) How many memory systems are there?, *American Psychologist,* 40(1), 385–98.

C

Coaching
Communication
Communities of practice
Constructivism
Continuing professional development
Curriculum

Coaching

Coaching is a developmental form of mentoring, as opposed to a judgemental model that assesses the performance of the mentees. The background to an interest in coaching and mentoring goes back to 'Success for All' in 2002 and exemplifies what Lawy and Tedder (2011: 385) identify as an attempt to introduce qualifications designed to meet the professional needs of individuals working in different educational contexts. The mentoring/coaching initiative appears to have been informed by the Ofsted reports of 2003, 2006, 2007, and 2008. Ofsted noted in 2003 that there was 'a lack of systematic mentoring and support in the workplace' (Ofsted, 2003: 2). In 2002, the White Paper *Further Education: Raising Skills, Improving Life Chances* (DfES, 2006) led to the introduction of a series of revised standards for the lifelong learning sector via LLUK (Lifelong Learning UK) that were more stringent than the previous FENTO (Further Education National Training Organisation) standards. This characteristic 'standards-driven' education (Lucas, 2007) emerged as an increasingly dominant characteristic within the lifelong learning sector. Lawy and Tedder (2011: 386) note that this led to the introduction of 'a plethora of National Awarding Body qualifications, from Preparing to Teach in the Lifelong Learning Sector (PTLLS) to the Diploma in Teaching in the Lifelong Learning Sector (DTLLS)'. Against this background of standards-driven educational initiatives, a discussion around mentoring models has emerged. In particular, there have been discussions about whether a 'coaching' (or 'nurturing') model should be applied within the lifelong learning context. Lawy and Tedder (2011: 386) note that the judgemental nature of Ofsted (as evidenced by the 2003 Ofsted report) has helped shape the nature of mentoring within the lifelong learning sector. Lawy and Tedder (2011: 386) go on to identify that the relatively 'ad hoc' nature of mentoring 'has been linked formally to college systems and structures including teacher training programmes'.

Alongside the emergence of this interventionist approach to providing mentors for trainee teachers and newly qualified teachers, there has appeared tension over the definition of mentoring. Hankey (2004), Ingleby and Tummons (2012), and Lawy and Tedder (2011: 389) identify that there are 'different definitions and models of mentoring' available for the professions. There are a number of public and private sector organisations – social services, the National Health Service (NHS), the Training and Development Agency (TDA), the European Mentoring and Coaching Council (EMCC), and the Chartered Institute of Personnel and Development (CIPD) – that use mentors. All of these organisations have a commitment to mentoring, but they have different understandings of the purpose of mentoring to the 'support and challenge' model preferred by Ofsted. In exemplifying this point, CIPD consider there to be three important parts in the mentoring relationship, as outlined by Alred *et al.* (1998): exploration, new understanding, and action planning. Lawy and Tedder (2011: 389) identify this particular mentoring process as being supportive of learning and development and more informal than coaching. Moreover, this model of mentoring enables individuals to manage their careers by developing professional skills alongside helping with personal issues. The key component of this mentoring model is that it is about developing capability as opposed to assessing competence with respect to performance and skills.

Tedder and Lawy (2009) outline, however, that since 2003 Ofsted has viewed mentoring in a highly judgemental way as opposed to viewing the mentoring process as developmental. The inspectorate appears to wish to assess the impact of mentoring on educational performance by measuring this performance against academic results. The variety of interpretation of the purpose of mentoring, however, reveals a difficulty with the Ofsted agenda (Tedder and Lawy, 2009). It seems highly unlikely that all stakeholders will accept unilaterally the 'support' and 'challenge' model of mentoring when other (more appealing) models of mentoring are available, such as coaching.

Communication

Communication is the transmission or passing on by speaking or writing – or through non-verbal means such as gesture – of ideas, attitudes or concepts. It might also involve the sharing of a feeling or understanding about a topic or issue. For teachers and trainers in a further education college or adult education centre, such a definition is immediately recognisable. Teachers talk with their students in a classroom, indicating agreement or acknow-ledging progress through a few carefully chosen words or through a nod or thumbs-up in the midst of a busy and noisy workshop, and offer constructive advice and guidance in a tutorial session accompanied by reassuring ges-tures such as a smile or a nod of the head.

In a learning and teaching environment, communication by the teacher or trainer is usually intended to influence the behaviour of the students in some way. This might be to direct attention to a specific task that requires comple-tion, to check prior learning through asking a series of questions, or to man-age *behaviour*. Different kinds or modes of communication might therefore be employed in these situations. Communication may be verbal or non-verbal, formal or informal, one-way or two-way. The primary function of communica-tion in a learning and teaching context is the establishment of a shared (by the teacher and the students) environment of discussion, practice, and work around the topic or issue being learned, practised or assessed.

The establishment of clear and unambiguous lines or channels of com-munication in the workshop or classroom does not only relate to the speech, or gesture, of the teacher, however. Any medium for communication that uses words and/or symbols (signs, pictures or photographs, for example) needs to be carefully constructed and evaluated. This might relate to something as sim-ple as a handout, or something more complicated such as a body of resources uploaded to a virtual learning environment (VLE). All such media ought to be carefully evaluated, ensuring that the tone and register of the text used is appropriate for the intended audience. Technical language or *jargon* ought to be unambiguously defined. Language and image use should be inclusive and non-discriminatory.

The effectiveness of communication in the classroom may be weakened in a number of other ways:

- Physical conditions, such as lighting, temperature and seating, may cause a distraction.
- A poorly set out room in which the teacher or students can neither see nor hear one another properly can impede communication. In such circumstances, the teacher should, as far as possible, rearrange the room so that open sight lines can be established between all of the members of the group.
- Poor choice or style of activity can impede communication. A long lecture instead of a workshop format, a presentation that is deliv-ered too rapidly, a lecturer who is visibly disinterested in the work that the students are engaging with, or a nervous disposition due to a lack of preparation on the part of the tutor can all create barriers to communication.

The importance of thinking about the ways in which teachers in the life-long learning sector communicate with their students cannot be underestimated. Teachers and trainers need to talk with their students and apprentices in different ways at different times: the context of a pastoral tutorial in which the teacher needs to provide additional support for a vulnerable student in a further education college, for example, is quite different to the context of a portfolio workshop in which the teacher is going through the assessment requirements for a module or unit of study for an adult student who is studying in the evening after a busy day at work. The teacher or trainer has to consider how she or he dresses or moves around the classroom, how the workshop is laid out, and which words or technical terms to employ, to ensure that communication is as clear and unambiguous as possible.

Communities of practice

A community of practice is a group of people who gather together in some way to do something. People engage in all kinds of activities – *practices* – as part of their 'everyday' lives, interacting with other people, sometimes in close proximity and sometimes at a distance or by proxy: at work, at play, with families or with friends. To take part in these various practices, people come together in *communities* so that they can talk about their practices, share them and learn more about them. These *communities of practice* can be found in formal, institutionalised settings and in informal ones such as adult learners in a basic skills class, teachers of mathematics, hairdressing apprentices and trainee further education teachers.

In some communities, members will meet and talk on a regular basis; in others, they will meet only infrequently. Some communities have existed for a long time, whereas others are relatively new. Some communities establish and sustain close relations with others, sharing aspects of their practice, while others are relatively self-sufficient. All communities of practice, however, irrespective of their size, their membership or their age, share specific structural qualities. There are three attributes that are described as maintaining the coherence of practice within a community (Wenger, 1998: 73–85):

- *Mutual engagement.* This is the term used to refer to the ways in which members of a community of practice interact with one another and do whatever they do. This might be face to face or via email, in a meeting or through a large social gathering. Because working together creates differences as well as similarities, differences and similarities of opinion or fact can be seen and heard.
- *Joint enterprise.* This is the term used to refer to the shared work or endeavour of the community of practice. The joint enterprise of a

community of practice can be seen as being the 'aim or 'focus' of the community.

- *Shared repertoire.* This is the term used to describe the habits, routines, tools, and other materials that over time have been created or adopted by a community of practice. Members of a community draw on the shared repertoire in order to engage in their practice.

According to communities of practice theory, learning is a consequence of engagement in practice (Lave and Wenger, 1991; Wenger, 1998). Thus, as people engage in practice, they learn about that practice at the same time; participation in a practice or activity always affords people the opportunity to learn about that practice; and people engage in practice in order to learn. People need to be allowed to participate at first in only a small way, before being allowed over time to engage more fully – a form of apprenticeship. Learning in this way changes how people think, act, and speak.

As members learn and therefore become more expert in the practice of their community over time, they draw on the repertoire, tools, and artefacts of the community in an increasingly expert manner. Their participation, within the community, becomes more full. But this does not imply that the time will eventually come when members have 'finished' learning. This is because communities of practice do not themselves remain still. In fact, they are constantly moving and changing. This might be because new ideas or tools come into a community from outside, causing the practice of the community to change. Or it might be because members of a community have new ideas or find new ways of working with existing tools or artefacts that cause the community to shift. As a result, a community of practice is never 'finished' or 'still. Consequently, the ways in which the members of the community move around and work are also never finished: there is always something new to do and therefore something new to learn.

Constructivism

Constructivism is an educational perspective that is associated with how knowledge is created by individuals. The philosophical origins of constructivism could be said to go back to Immanuel Kant's Copernican revolution of philosophical thought (Audi, 1995). As opposed to asking 'big' questions like 'Is there a God?' and 'How are we made?', Kant was more concerned with how individuals interpret these 'big' questions. An emphasis is placed on our individual interpretation of the world and our unique understanding of God. Constructivism is at the centre of experiential learning with its emphasis on practical exploratory education. It is opposed to didactic teaching and is exemplified in many of the learning activities that occur within the lifelong learning sector. Constructivism is associated with several educationalists, including John Dewey, Maria Montessori and David Kolb:

- John Dewey's creation of an active learning laboratory at the end of the nineteenth century is an early example of constructivism. Dewey explored ways of enhancing active or experiential learning. He placed an emphasis on education that expands thinking and reflection. Interaction with the environment is considered to be a key element within active learning.
- An Italian educationalist, Maria Montessori emphasised the importance of practical learning. As an example, learning as a result of memorising facts is replaced with practical interactive learning. 'Props' or practical objects are used to 'construct' learning.
- David Kolb emphasises experiential learning. Kolb explores the importance of learning through 'concrete experience', learning through 'observation–reflection', the construction of abstract concepts, and testing in new situations. Kolb's model of learning can be visualised as a continuous spiral of learning.

The lifelong learning sector is often associated with constructivism because many of the traditional subject areas are vocational and practical. The inspirational vision generated by Maria Montessori has seen nontraditional learners achieving incredible feats of learning due to the merits of practical learning by doing. This, in turn, has led to the generation of a learning climate embracing practical kinaesthetic learning activities. Despite the popularity of constructivism there are criticisms of this educational perspective. Not all learners are able to construct knowledge. Educationalists such as Vygotsky argue that the schemata that are necessary for experiential learning need to have been generated. It is necessary to establish firm foundations for learning before we utilise experiential learning. Moreover, there are learners who do not enjoy constructivist learning methods. They may respond better to didactic teaching because this fits with their learning preference. An example of this can be seen with Montessori's approach to classroom displays. In many classrooms in the lifelong learning sector, visual displays adorn the classroom. Many teaching staff, learners and parents enjoy seeing these displays of learning. Yet Montessori was opposed to such classroom displays. Instead of constructing learning for the learners, the learners were expected to construct learning by themselves. It can be argued that it is only a certain type of learner who is able to do this. Learners who lack originality and inventiveness are not always able to construct meaning. This necessitates the use of other types of learning strategy alongside constructivism. There is no single learning perspective that is able to meet every learner's needs. Constructivism is like other learning perspectives – it is interesting and relevant to some but not all learners. If it is combined with other educational perspectives to form as holistic an approach as possible, its application can be highly useful for the lifelong learning sector.

Continuing professional development

Continuing professional development (CPD) refers to the training that is given to professional staff. In the lifelong learning sector, the Institute for Learning (IfL) advocates that teaching staff ought to do 30 hours of CPD each year to maintain currency of practice. This recommendation may be regarded as either a positive or a negative development, depending on one's interpretation of the educational benefits of the recommendation:

- If the lifelong learning sector is perceived to be a sector of education that is associated with change and fluidity, it is understandable to ask staff to commit to CPD. This will enable teaching staff to meet the needs of a diverse range of learners. In this respect, the IfL recommendation can be regarded as a good initiative.
- If, however, one asks about the process that has led to the recommendation for 30 hours of CPD becoming accepted as a part of the remit of staff in the lifelong learning sector, a different interpretation of this initiative is possible. Is this an example of professional development that is driven by the teaching staff in the lifelong learning sector or an example of 'top-down' managerialism?

Continuing professional development is regarded in general as being an important aspect of professional education. The reflective practice that enables teachers to improve their teaching can be enabled as a result of CPD. In the UK, organisations such as the International Professional Development Association (IPDA) have devoted conferences and academic journal articles to exploring the benefits of CPD in education. A number of significant benefits have resulted from IPDA's work. An accepted group of academics is involved in IPDA and they have been able to critique policy initiatives in terms of their development of professional practice (or otherwise). Academics (including Mathias Urban) have used IPDA to publicise the developmental areas within the UK education system. Urban (2008) argues that it is important to unite what he refers to as 'ways of being' (teaching and learning) with 'ways of knowing' (or policies about teaching and learning). The argument developed by Urban about education in the UK is that there can be a separation of policy and practice. One possible explanation for this separation of teaching policy and practice is that the policy makers have not had extensive experience of being educators.

The advantage of organisations like IPDA is that they are able to challenge some of the current CPD initiatives. The academic journal produced by IPDA (*Professional Development in Education*) includes research articles about CPD. Many of the articles reflect on the merits or otherwise of CPD at national and international level. Some of the mentor training programmes in the lifelong learning sector have been researched and commented on by academics in *Professional Development in Education* (e.g. Ingleby and Tummons, 2012). The work of organisations such as IPDA enables the UK to have a vibrant commitment to CPD as long as the economic circumstances of the country are perceived to support such initiatives. In recent years, the Coalition government's interpretation of the economic recession has meant that many CPD initiatives are under threat due to funding shortages. This may in turn impact upon the teaching profession and its ability to reflect upon how to enhance ways of teaching and learning in the future.

Curriculum

Definitions of curriculum can be understood as consisting of three key elements. First, there is *course content*, the specified content of a unit or programme of study that has been agreed, normally by an awarding or examining body, as describing the knowledge, ability or skill that students will acquire or accomplish as a consequence of participation. The second key element is *assessment and accreditation*, processes by which the extent of the student's learning can be evaluated against predetermined criteria that are derived from the curriculum content. The third key element is the *teaching staff*: if a curriculum is to be successfully delivered, it needs to be by a suitably qualified professional educator or other professional who has recognised training or teaching expertise.

Researchers offer a number of other definitions of curriculum. Concepts such as the planned curriculum and the received curriculum, which make a distinction between the ways a curriculum is planned and specified and the ways in which it is delivered and experienced in the workshop or seminar room, raise important questions about how educational curricula are delivered across different institutions. Concepts such as the total curriculum define curriculum as including everything that is needed to allow a curriculum to be enacted: not only programmes of study, but also people (teaching staff, academic support staff), infrastructure (systems, routines), admissions policies, artefacts (textbooks, virtual learning platforms), and even buildings (Kelly, 2009). The impact of this broader conceptualisation of curriculum is contestable. It is patently difficult to standardise buildings (as any comparison between a 'new build' further education college and an older college building from, say, the 1950s makes clear), although curricular authorities commonly audit the provision of sufficient and appropriate technical and vocational equipment for the delivery of the vocational curriculum in colleges and workplace or adult education settings. But it is more straightforward to attempt to standardise people through practices such as a requirement for mandatory qualifications (although for FE teachers this has recently been abolished) or through other human resource management strategies such as compulsory staff training (Garrick, 1998).

Perhaps the most widely recognised use of the term is in relation to course content. But in this way, again, we can discern several distinct meanings. The term 'vocational curriculum' can be seen as relating to course content, and encompassing course provision ranging from qualifications in brickwork to animal husbandry, beauty therapy to travel and tourism – all commonly found within the wider FE sector. But if it is contrasted with the term 'academic curriculum', arguments about the parity of vocational and academic qualifications, and the very different ways in which each is valued at a political and societal level, quickly emerge. By contrast, the 'functional skills' curriculum relates quite narrowly to the provision of numeracy and literacy teaching either on a stand-alone basis, or embedded across other curriculum areas, while the term 'motor vehicle curriculum' focuses on a specific occupational area, accompanied by links to industry and to a national set of occupational standards.

An important principle of curriculum provision is that the way in which a student experiences the curriculum should be comparable to the experience of any other student who is engaged in the same programme, but at a different college. Students need to be satisfied that they are not being disadvantaged through having chosen to study at one institution as opposed to another. Employers need to be satisfied that potential employees' qualifications, or other forms of professional endorsement, are trustworthy. Professions and industries need to be confident that entrants to those professions do indeed have all of the required knowledge and competence that their qualifications purport to represent. And funding agencies need to be satisfied that public money is being spent appropriately, according to current policy (Tummons, 2011).

References and further reading

Alred, G., Garvey, B. and Smith, R. (1998) *Mentoring Pocketbook.* Alresford: Management Pocketbooks.

Audi, R. (1995) *The Cambridge Dictionary of Philosophy.* Cambridge: Cambridge University Press.

Department for Education and Skills (DfES) (2006) *Further Education: Raising Skills, Improving Life Chances.* Norwich: The Stationery Office.

Garrick, J. (1998) *Informal Learning in the Workplace: Unmasking Human Resource Development.* London: Routledge.

Hankey, J. (2004) The good, the bad and other considerations: reflections on mentoring trainee teachers in post-compulsory education, *Research in Post-Compulsory Education*, 9(3), 389–400.

Ingleby, E. and Tummons, J. (2012) Repositioning professionalism: teachers, mentors, policy and praxis, *Research in Post-Compulsory Education*, 17(2), 163–79.

Kelly, A.V. (2009) *The Curriculum: Theory and Practice* (6th edn.). London: Sage.

Lave, J. and Wenger, E. (1991) *Situated Learning*. Cambridge: Cambridge University Press.

Lawy, R. and Tedder, M. (2011) Mentoring and individual learning plans: issues of practice in a period of transition, *Research in Post-Compulsory Education*, 16(3), 385–96.

Lucas, N. (2007) The in-service training of adult literacy, numeracy and English for Speakers of Other Languages teachers in England: the challenges of a 'standards-led model, *Journal of In-Service Education*, 33(2), 125–42.

Office for Standards in Education (Ofsted) (2003) *The Initial Training of Further Education Teachers in England: A Survey*. London: HMSO.

Tedder, M. and Lawy, R. (2009) The pursuit of 'excellence': mentoring in further education initial teacher training in England, *Journal of Vocational Education and Training*, 61(4), 413–29.

Tummons, J. (2011) *Curriculum Studies in the Lifelong Learning Sector* (2nd edn.). Exeter: Learning Matters.

Urban, M. (2008) Dealing with uncertainty: challenges and possibilities for the early childhood profession, *European Early Childhood Education Research Journal*, 16(2), 135–52.

Wenger, E. (1998) *Communities of Practice*. Cambridge: Cambridge University Press.

D

Development
Differentiation
Disabilities
Distance learning
Diversity
Dual professionalism

Development

Development is associated with the progress in learning that occurs as a result of the education process. Development needs to be measured if we are to be certain that an individual has made progress. The way that development is assessed and measured is a controversial area within the lifelong learning sector. The indicators used are frequently based on performance and achievement. If an individual achieves what are identified as 'key goals', this in turn is equated with 'development'. The controversy arises if this assessment of development is associated with narrow curriculum areas such as English, maths or ICTs. Our understanding of individual development links to psychology. The ideas within the behaviourist, psychodynamic and cognitive schools of psychology are frequently associated with exploring how individuals develop:

The rise of behaviourism. Malim and Birch (1998: 8) argue that by 1920 the behaviourist school of psychology had risen to prominence. John B. Watson was one of several theorists who believed that it was wrong to focus upon introspection because this approach to studying psychology is not measurable and thus invalidated its scientific credentials. Consequently, Watson dedicated himself to the study of what has become known as 'behaviourism', or human behaviour that is measurable and observable. Behaviourism remained the dominant force in psychology over the next 30 years, especially in the USA. Emphasis was placed on identifying the external factors that influenced human development.

Psychodynamic psychology. A criticism of behaviourism developed through the twentieth century as a result of the legacy of Sigmund Freud, possibly the most famous psychologist of all. Malim and Birch (1998: 9) argue that Freud proposed that the mind is a combination of conscious and unconscious thoughts. If we accept that this is the case, Freud's theory can be used to challenge behaviourism because it implies that human thought and behaviour are more complex than the behaviourist notion that external variables cause thought and behaviour. The development of the individual emerges as more of a focus than a study of the factors influencing individual development.

Cognitive psychology. Alongside psychodynamic theory emerged another theory that places the emphasis on thinking processes or cognition, in other words the ways in which we attain, retain and regain information. Within cognitive psychology, the focus is on identifying what happens within the mind after a stimulus has been received. The mind is seen as being like an information processor, almost akin to a computer. Malim and Birch (1998: 25) explain this perspective by arguing that 'human beings are seen as information processors who absorb information from the outside world, code and interpret it, store and retrieve it'. In a literal revolution of thought, thinking has come full circle and the initial criticism of introspection as being unlikely to explain the complexity of human thought is asserted within this psychological theory.

Biological psychology. Biological psychology has been discussed due to some of the current developments within psychology. The scientific advances of the 1990s and beyond in relation to identifying the genetic and hormonal composition of the human mind have generated enormous interest in the idea that thoughts, behaviour and human development are determined by our biology. This may be considered to be a reductionist argument because it reduces complex thoughts and behaviour to a few variables such as hormones and genes. The ideas within biological psychology may prove to be yet another passing paradigm contributing to the ongoing dialogue about human development.

Differentiation

Differentiation is understood as meeting the differing needs of learners. According to Petty (2009), the idea of a teacher being like a 'sage on a stage' is a dated idea; teachers in the lifelong learning sector are now equated with being 'guides on the side'. By this, Petty means that the traditional notion of teachers being accepted purely due to their position of authority has changed. There is an expectation that teachers will be supportive of the needs of their students. This has led to a rise in interest in differentiation.

The idea of differentiation is especially relevant for the lifelong learning sector because:

1.   The lifelong learning sector is associated with a range of learners learning different skills. It is entirely natural to assume that this diverse range of learners are likely to learn in very different ways. As opposed to expecting students to do what the teacher says, there is a new expectation that learning materials will be adapted for the needs of the students.
2.   Since the 1990s, Ofsted has placed an emphasis on trying to ensure that as many diverse learners as possible are included within the life-long learning sector. This agenda has formed part of New Labour's attempt to broaden access to education to as many non-traditional learners as possible.

Differentiation can be seen as a good initiative within the lifelong learning sector if as many learners as possible are having their learning needs met. The traditional style of learning that is very much teacher centred has needed to change to meet a diverse community of learners. If different learning tasks are meeting the needs of these students, this is a highly useful development. The rationale that is used behind how and why these different needs are being met has interested critics of differentiation including Coffield *et al.* (2004). These academics have questioned the rationale that is being used as a basis for dif-ferentiation. The concept of differentiation appears to have metamorphosed into the notion that there are different ways of learning and different types of learner. Coffield *et al.* (2004) suggest that this obvious point can have quite radical implications for the curriculum. Like the analogy 'the tail wagging the dog', is it worthwhile adapting the curriculum in a radical way to meet the needs of a diverse number of different learners? Is it not a reasonable expec-tation that learners should learn in a way that maintains traditional values?

The advantage of the debate about differentiation appears to be that the role of the lifelong learning sector has been strengthened. It is accepted that the curriculum ought to include as many learners as possible so that their needs are met. The debate over differentiation has also led to the defence of good practice in teaching. There is raised awareness of the importance of appropriate learning models to meet the needs of learners. Schwandt (2004) draws attention to the importance of accepting that education is often involved with 'the messiness of human life'. It is not possible to avoid life's difficulties through assuming that differentiated learning can reach every learner all the time. Perhaps there ought to be acceptance of the merits and shortcomings of differentiation so that educational achievement can be realised in a sensible and balanced way, as opposed to assuming that differentiated learning is the answer to every question.

Disabilities

The proportion of students with disabilities is increasing. For example, the proportion of students with disabilities in higher education rose from 7.8 per cent to 8.5 per cent between 2000 and 2004 (Higher Education Academy, 2005). In the lifelong learning sector, many learners experience challenges integrating into formal learning and teaching. Owing to the social and environmental barriers experienced by these learners, teaching staff face many challenges facilitating learning with these students. As a result of the needs of these learners, there are a number of considerations that ought to be made in respect of learning and inclusive practice. These considerations can depend on whether or not the learners are expected to follow the formal national curriculum. According to Malcolm Knowles (1989, cited in Tennant, 1997), education relies on a range of assumptions about the learning process. A key assumption is that the best form of learning occurs when learners become self-directed and motivated so that there is autonomy over the learning process. This approach is adopted to ensure that the learners become interested in the curriculum. This particular approach to learning emphasises the importance of 'social skills' within the learning process and their relation to 'motivation'. Motivation can be regarded as being potentially intrinsic or extrinsic to the learning process. Whether motivation is intrinsic or extrinsic in orientation can have an impact upon the success or otherwise of the curriculum. 'Generally, intrinsic interest in a subject is typically associated with high levels of intrinsic motivation and this in turn is linked to successful learning/achievement outcomes' (Brown *et al.*, 1998: 16). Extrinsic motivation is associated with factors outside or external to the individual. Brown and colleagues (1998: 16) state that 'learners who are extrinsically motivated are influenced by external rewards and pressures. Learners who have high extrinsically motivating factors can feel "controlled" by them and this can have a negative impact on their intrinsic motivation.' Educationally, intrinsic motivation (or intrinsic interest in the subject) is seen as being the most desirable type of motivation to promote learning, as it leads to 'deep learning' approaches and learning outcomes that are 'concerned with conceptual understanding of the material, and incorporating this into one's existing knowledge' (Fry *et al.*, 2003: 65). However, it is generally acknowledged that learners who have strong extrinsically motivating factors will still do what is necessary to 'please the teacher'. This form of 'strategic learning' may not always lead to deep learning, so if we consider how to meet the needs of learners with disabilities, how can we develop a curriculum that is inclusive and provides the best opportunities and motivation for learning?

It may be worth developing individual learning plans for these learners and including SMART (specific, measurable, achievable, relevant and time-bound) targets for learning. It is important to consider individuals' needs, abilities, preferred ways of learning, appropriate learning targets and preferred methods of assessment. It may be that individual learning plans are reviewed on a one-to-one basis with the tutor. This type of approach to providing an inclusive curriculum can be considered to be one of the best approaches for enhancing learning, as it is a means of responding to the individual needs of the learners. As opposed to focusing on national targets and a national curriculum, this approach to enhancing learning attempts to adapt the curriculum according to the individual needs of the students. If this way of enhancing learning is characterised by structuring and planning within the learning process, it becomes possible to develop strategies for measuring the learning that has taken place with learners who have disabilities.

Students who combine practical and academic learning tasks in the classroom have an opportunity to access a more vocational curriculum. This often means that they have the opportunity to develop a variety of skills. The curriculum planned for this group of learners is likely to require thought and consideration. Owing to the wide range of disability, it is important to ensure that the individual needs of learners are met. When planning an inclusive programme for these learners, it is important to ensure that there is an appropriate balance of knowledge, skills, and practical development for each learner.

Distance learning

Distance learning is an example of flexible learning. As opposed to a traditional form of learning where learners are taught in a conventional classroom environment throughout the academic year, distance learning is characterised by the learners not always being physically present with the teaching staff. It may be that learners attend the lifelong learning setting some of the time but return to where they live and work and continue their learning there. A number of examples of distance learning programmes can be seen in the lifelong learning sector. The 'HE in FE' programmes are one example in which this type of learning occurs. In one programme, a degree in podiatry was taught in Ireland and Canada by a host lifelong learning sector organisation in the UK. The students attended the lifelong learning sector organisation for their induction but were then expected to take a collection of learning resources home with them to complete formative assessments online. The summative assessment within the programme was completed with just one week of attendance at the host centre!

The popularity of distance learning programmes has increased due to the rise of the Internet. It is now possible to have 'virtual teaching' and online marking. The realisation that education has a commercial value has also influenced the rise in distance learning. Qualifications can be offered to cohorts of students in other countries via online teaching. There are benefits to distance learning, such as the curriculum is made to appear flexible and innovative.

This may appeal to non-traditional learners who may not achieve within a conventional classroom environment. Part of the appeal of distance learning to the lifelong learning sector is that it is an example of the non-traditional learning that the sector has traditionally represented. The wish to make the curriculum as innovative as possible is another benefit of distance learning. Petty (2009) draws attention to the importance of ensuring that the curriculum becomes tailored to the needs of individuals. An example of this adapted curriculum appears with distance learning.

There are also disadvantages with distance learning. For example, to be successful the learning process may depend upon close contact between learners and teachers, something that is lost with distance learning. Some learners require encouragement and explanation through classroom contact as opposed to interacting online. Petty (2009) also draws attention to the discipline that is involved in study. It takes time, effort, commitment, and sheer determination to learn. It can be difficult to achieve this learning in an online forum. The social side to learning, with its scaffolding that is associated with Bruner and Vygotsky, is also not as easy to facilitate with distance learning. In a classroom context, it is possible to 'learn from the group'. This learning scaffold can emerge as a vital component of the learning process. With distance learning, the learner experiences a more isolated or virtual experience of learning. It is also important not simply to follow what is held as being right because it is regarded as being 'novel' or 'original'. Distance learning may be seen as representing something of a learning *Zeitgeist* because it uses technology. As a number of critics of learning through technology have noted, the most important process is what is being learnt and not the application of technology due to the misguided belief that 'e is best' (Karamarski and Feldman, 2000; Marsh *et al.*, 2005; Leask and Younie, 2013).

Diversity

Diversity is a term that is associated with the vast array of learners who are part of the lifelong learning sector. Our raised awareness of diversity in the UK is a result of legislation that has drawn attention to the many varied learners who are part of the lifelong learning sector. The Disability Discrimination Act (DDA) was passed in 1995, was extended in 2002 and amended in 2005. The original legislation was passed to protect disabled people from discrimination and defined disability as follows: 'a person has a disability if he or she has a physical or mental impairment, which has a substantial and long-term adverse effect on his/her ability to carry out normal day to day activities'.

In 2001, the Special Educational Needs and Disability Act (2001), also known as SENDA (Part 4 of the DDA), brought education into the remit of the Disability Discrimination Act. This extension, which was implemented in

September 2002, ensures that disabled learners are treated no less favourably than any other learners. The Act uses a broader spectrum in defining disability as the legislation refers to: 'people with physical or sensory impairments, dyslexia, medical conditions, mental health difficulties and learning difficulties'.

The 2002 extension to the Act is particularly important for those in the lifelong learning sector, as it relates directly to educational organisations. It is important for teachers in schools to anticipate the needs of children with disabilities as opposed to responding to the needs of children in their educational context.

As a result of this legislation, it is deemed to be desirable that educational organisations have in place the mechanisms to encourage the disclosure of disabilities. The ideal aim is for adjustments to be made prior to learners joining the programme, which may be done via the recruitment and interview process. Following the 2002 extension to the Act, many organisations offering educational programmes reviewed their recruitment and interview procedures. These reviews were completed in order to encourage applicants to disclose disabilities that could impact upon their educational progress prior to joining educational programmes. However, according to Tummons (2011: 100), it is important to bear in mind that learners 'are not obliged to tell anyone they have a disability' and that 'it is possible for a learner with a disability to feel that they have been discriminated against even if they have not revealed the disability'.

Tummons goes on to indicate that the legislation is there to provide a framework for teachers to work within and that this framework should be liberating and not oppressive. At all times, it is important not to lose sight of the concept of 'reasonableness' when adapting buildings or practice. Tummons (2011: 100) indicates some areas of practice where adjustments should be made, such as 'adjustments to the exterior of buildings, to course materials, to assessment practices and to classrooms and workshops'. Tummons also emphasises that trainee teachers should not feel isolated when they are planning a curriculum of inclusivity. It is important to ensure that all available support mechanisms are used, such as seeking specialist advice from learning difficulty and disability coordinators. Other sources of support may include practice mentors, other more experienced teachers, awarding bodies, and external support networks such as action groups for the disabled. The learners themselves should always be at the centre of the process and, where possible, their guidance should be sought as to meeting their needs.

Dual professionalism

New teachers and trainers in the lifelong learning sector invariably enter the profession with a variety of qualifications relating to their technical, vocational or occupational specialisms, but rarely with a professional teaching qualification as well. Over four-fifths of trainee teachers in lifelong learning study for their teaching qualifications on a part-time, in-service basis. For new teachers and trainers who are working full time in a further education college, becoming an educator represents a second career. But many new practitioners begin on a part-time, hourly-paid basis: this is not uncommon in further education colleges and is particularly widespread in adult and community education.

As such, any attempt to define the professional identity of teachers and trainers in the lifelong learning sector is far from straightforward. Many new full-time teachers continue to identify strongly with their trade or commercial background: they define themselves primarily as 'plasterers' or 'electrical installers', rather than 'teachers of plastering' or 'teachers of electrical installation'. Part-time teachers often continue to work in their specialist area – for them, teaching is considered an 'add-on' to an existing occupation. Many of those who are new to teaching in the sector will therefore continue, more or less implicitly, to derive their professional identity and thus their professional behaviour, from the world of work. There are several elements to this. They might derive their behaviour in informal ways, perhaps from the social and cultural contexts of their specialism; this might become apparent in the language that they use or the patterns of dress that they employ. Or it might be a more formal process, perhaps bound up in the codes of conduct or occupational standards that govern the industry in question.

Questions relating to the ways in which teachers and trainers see or position themselves are usually explored in terms of the concept of dual professionalism. This is a concept that foregrounds the background of the teacher or trainer, recognising that many new entrants to teaching in the lifelong learning sector already possess considerable experience, knowledge, and aptitude. At one level, therefore, the dual professionalism model can be seen as serving the interests of the teaching workforce, allowing as it does the existing expertise of the individual teacher to be recognised and acknowledged. It also provides a space for the occupational expertise of the teacher to be sustained and enhanced in the future. Just as the workshops in a further education college ought to be equipped to meet current trade and industry specifications (after all, there is little point in having college students learn using outmoded tools and materials), so the teaching staff ought to maintain currency, to ensure that their knowledge, aptitude, and skills are up to date and reflect current, and not redundant, business or industry practices. Sustaining a dual professionalism requires the teacher – and hence the employer – to plan for relevant trade and industry updating and development, in addition to training as a teacher.

The counter-argument is that a model of dual professionalism serves to diminish the very teacher professionalism that ought to be encouraged through not only the completion of an initial professional qualification but also through subsequent continuing professional development. From this perspective, dual professionalism acts to take attention away from the professional ethos of the teacher, which, in the further education sector is – arguably – already only weakly framed (and made weaker by the recent decision, at the time of writing, to reintroduce voluntarism into the education of teachers in the sector). For those commentators who seek to explore and inform an ethic or philosophy of teaching, it is by no means the case that the professional ethics of teaching are sufficiently closely related to those of many of the occupational areas represented in the further education curriculum, so that it can be assumed that they are straightforwardly transferable.

References and further reading

Brown, S., Armstrong, A. and Thompson, G. (1998) *Motivating Students*. Birmingham: SEDA Publications.

Coffield, F., Moseley, D., Hall, E. and Ecclestone, K. (2004) *Should We be Using Learning Styles? What Research has to Say to Practice*. London: Learning and Skills Research Centre.

Fry, H., Ketteridge, S. and Marshall, S. (2003) *A Handbook for Teaching and Learning in Higher Education* (2nd edn.). London: Routledge Falmer.

Higher Education Academy (2005) *Disability Legislation: A Practical Guide for Academics*. London: Equality Challenge Unit.

Karamarski, B. and Feldman, Y. (2000) Internet in the classroom: effects on reading, comprehension and metacognition, *Educational Media International*, 37(3), 149–55.

Leask, M. and Younie, S. (2013) National models for continuing professional development: the challenges of twenty first-century knowledge management, *Professional Development in Education*, 39(2), 273–87.

Malim, T. and Birch, A. (1998) *Introductory Psychology*. London: Hodder & Stoughton.

Marsh, J., Brooks, G., Hughes, J., Ritchie, L., Roberts, S. and Wright, K. (2005) *Digital Beginnings: Young People's Use of Popular Culture, New Media and New Technologies*. Sheffield: University of Sheffield.

Orr, K. and Simmons, R. (2010) Dual identities: the in-service teacher trainee experience in the English further education sector, *Journal of Vocational Education and Training*, 62(1), 75–88.

Petty, G. (2009) *Teaching Today* (4th edn.). Cheltenham: Nelson Thornes.

Schwandt, T.A. (2004) Hermeneutics: a poetics of inquiry versus a methodology for research, in H. Piper and I. Stronach (eds.) *Educational Research: Difference and Diversity*. Aldershot: Ashgate.

Tennant, M. (1997) *Psychology and Adult Education* (2nd edn.). London: Routledge.

Tummons, J. (2011) *Curriculum Studies in the Lifelong Learning Sector* (2nd edn.). Exeter: Learning Matters.

E

Edutainment
E-learning
Employability
Empowerment
Experiential learning

Edutainment

Edutainment (educational entertainment or education through entertainment) refers to the use of entertainment media in order to educate, such as through television or radio programmes. More recently, it has also come to be used to describe the educational use of other objects or media such as toys or computers, in reference not only to objects that have been designed with an educational purpose in mind but also to objects that have been designed in the first instance for entertainment purposes, but which have been redeployed in or repurposed for educational settings. The use of the term has been further extended to include the use of classroom resources or techniques that mimic activities or objects that might be recognised by students as being derived from entertainment media.

Materials or resources designed with an educational purpose in mind, but also to be played as games, for example, are readily observed within the lifelong learning sector. Many of the Standards Unit's teaching and learning resources produced by the then Department for Education and Skills (many of these blue boxes of resources are still being used in colleges and adult education centres) include board-based games and card-sort games. Computer programs for use with basic skills learners are another example; the software applications that accompany interactive whiteboards provide a third. Activities and resources such as these are well established in the lifelong learning sector.

Objects that have been designed initially for entertainment purposes, but which can be used for educational purposes, are equally varied in scope.

Some examples of edutainment resources and strategies of this kind are relatively straightforward, such as the use of YouTube videos in the workshop or classroom (although care should always be taken to ensure that the video is of good enough quality for viewing on a large screen, as well as being of meaningful value – all too often, video is used to fill time rather than engage learning). Others are more complex, but also (arguably) more worthwhile. The use of Lego for 'serious play' is a standout example: Lego models (ranging from relatively inexpensive simple bricks to complex programmable robotic models) have been used within the social sciences, sciences, and engineering, in both formal educational institutions and in organisational work-based learning (Frick *et al.*, 2013). More complex again is the use of mainstream computer games for learning, an area in which much research has been conducted relating to language and literacy learning through playing computer games (Gee, 2004, 2005).

Classroom techniques that mimic entertainment formats, such as allowing students to take part in a 'who wants to be a millionaire' style of multiple-choice, question-and-answer session (this can be done using interactive whiteboards, or using other proprietary ICT hardware and software such as Qwizdom or PowerPoint) are less straightforward to evaluate. This is because their effectiveness as tools for learning has not been subject to any serious educational research, although any question-and-answer format such as this will be restricted in terms of the complexity or subtlety of the questions that can be asked, and hence the learning that can be assessed.

'Edutainment', at one level, can be seen to be applicable to a range of practices – of pedagogies – that are serious and that are based on a meaningful engagement with theory and research. It is also used as a term of mild opprobrium, particularly in relation to 'gimmicky' activities that are seen to add little to classroom practice but which have been positioned (rightly or wrongly) as the 'kinds' of activity needed to engage students who might otherwise be at risk of leaving education – an attitude that is both mistaken and patronising.

E-learning

Jones (1980: 33) identifies 1980 as a key date in the sustained government involvement in 'e-learning' (or electronic learning). Before 1980, Selwyn (2011: 396) notes, there was little application of digital technology in educational settings with the exception of some occasional application of 'microcomputing'. This situation changed with the Conservative government from 1979 onwards. Margaret Thatcher's administration established policies that led to microcomputers being introduced 'so that our young people are skilled at an early age' (Thatcher, 1983). This led to the increase of technology within education in the UK.

The establishment of the National Council for Educational Technology continued this emerging use of technology in education and, by the end of the 1980s, e-learning was firmly entrenched within the National Curriculum. Clegg *et al.* (2010) acknowledge that this led to the role of the computer within education becoming accepted at a 'political' level.

The election to power of New Labour in 1997 coincided with the emergence of the Internet and the World Wide Web. This led to computers becoming an important part of public and private life. The political discourse at this time reveals the heightened importance of computers within educational policy. In 2000, David Blunkett gave a speech at Greenwich University in which e-learning was presented as a 'seismic' component of the elements of globalisation. In this speech, Blunkett presented globalisation as a consequence of new forms of communication by claiming that 'money moves around the globe at the click of a button, and the sums are huge'. The Blair and Brown administrations pursued a series of sustained educationally focused programmes for developing technology. Three distinct phases of policymaking followed. From 1998 to 2002, the National Grid for Learning (NGfL) was established. From 2002 to 2005, ICT in schools emerged as a key educational policy, and from 2005 to 2010 the 'Harnessing Technology' agenda embellished the government's approach to e-learning.

These three policies were supported by a number of other developments. The National Council for Educational Technology was expanded and developed into the British Educational Communications and Technology Agency (BECTA). This 'quango' became responsible for the development of e-learning in education as a renewed emphasis was placed on the importance of technology in education.

By 2010, New Labour had essentially combined political commitment to technology in schools. In contrast, technology was conspicuous by its absence in the manifestos of the opposition parties in the 2010 election. The Conservatives and Liberal Democrats chose to say very little about ICTs during the election campaign. This represented a significant change in direction from the earlier position adopted by the Conservative Party. This new approach of being quiet about educational technology contrasted significantly with New Labour's policy approach in this area. Moreover, the formation of the Coalition government led to the closing of BECTA as the new government began engaging immediately in what political commentators referred to as the 'bonfire of the quangos' (Selwyn, 2011). BECTA was closed after the formation of the new government, with a loss of 250 staff and a budget of £80 million.

In response to the popular claim that austerity was required to 'balance the books', the Coalition government reversed New Labour's plans to emphasise the importance of digital technology as a key component of teaching and learning. The exploration of 'web 2.0' technologies and 'digital technologies' was forgotten in a notion of 'saving money at all costs'. This change of policy direction was not an anti-technology stance but based on the perceived need for funding cuts.

Employability

Employability is the term used to gather together and describe those skills that employers expect students to acquire while at college in order to prepare them for the world of work. The definition of 'skills' that is proposed by notions such as 'employability skills' is generic, seeing skills as something that can be acquired in a variety of ways and applied to different employment or educational contexts. That is, employability skills are transferable. A typical list of the kinds of attribute that are defined as employability skills might include (Thomas and Jones, 2007: 22):

- creativity
- flexibility
- willingness to learn
- autonomy
- working in a team
- ability to manage others
- ability to work under pressure
- good oral communication
- good written communication
- numeracy
- attention to detail
- good time management skills
- ability to make decisions.

At first glance, a list of skills such as these would seem to be uncontroversial. However, meaningful criticisms of the 'employability agenda' continue to be put forward. And even though employers consistently complain that too many college leavers lack the right employability skills, they continue to give more jobs to people with academic qualifications than vocational ones (Allen and Ainley, 2007). Employability skills are positioned at an individual level: a student having the skills, knowledge, attitudes and behaviours required to look for, gain, and maintain employment in the labour market can be seen as 'employable'. In this sense, employability is positioned as an individual characteristic. The responsibility is on the individual to take responsibility for their education and training and by extension for their economic and social well-being – it is not the direct responsibility of the state.

There are two issues here. The first is the extent to which employability skills are indeed transferable. For many occupations, specific qualifications are obviously necessary. Becoming a nursery worker requires more than just a range of generic qualifications and good results in functional skills tests – it requires specific qualifications and experience. A student on a business studies course might consider a range of possible employment options on completion of their studies. But going to work for a credit card insurance company in a call centre will surely require quite different skills from going to work as an office junior for a high street firm of solicitors, simply because they are two such different employment contexts. The second issue relates to the individual capacity of the student. Put simply, if a student successfully completes her or his programme of study – and as such can be said to be 'employable' – but fails to find employment, what happens next? Will she or he need to undergo more training, to become 'more' employable? What is the relationship between college course provision and local opportunities for employment?

The lifelong learning sector can be said to contribute to the employability agenda in two ways, therefore. First, the sector provides courses that allow employability skills to develop within the curriculum. Further education colleges in particular can be effective in bringing the world of work 'into the classroom', through the provision of realistic working environments such as training salons, and through the organisation of work placements and such like. Second, the sector provides specialist provision (such as entry to employment) that purports to address the skills that young people need to find work. But significant concerns can be raised as to the quality of such provision and the extent to which the employability skills that they deliver are aligned to the world of work, as recent research indicates that specific 'employability' programmes lead only to unskilled or low-skilled work characterised by low pay, low status, and low job security.

Empowerment

Empowerment is often associated with humanism and the work of Carl Rogers (1902–1987). Rogers emphasises the importance of the individual interpretation of external factors. As opposed to emphasising the importance of external variables, attention is given to the importance of individuals interpreting social reality. Humanism can be associated with the philosophy of Immanuel Kant and his 'Copernican revolution' of thought (Audi, 1995: 400). As opposed to asking about the reality of the universe, Kant changes the focus of the argument to ask about how individuals understand social reality. Humanism asks a similar question. Instead of focusing upon how external variables produce thoughts, the humanist emphasis is on how individuals make sense of external variables.

Humanism has also become associated with the work of Abraham Maslow. Maslow proposes that all humans have a 'hierarchy of needs' and that individual thoughts are influenced by the extent to which these physiological and intellectual needs are being met. Carl Rogers has had a particularly important influence on humanism and it may be claimed that Rogers is the founding father of psychological humanism. His work is also influential in what is considered as being effective teaching practice. One of the most important Rogerian ideas to have influenced the lifelong learning sector is the proposal that anxiety is a product of what has become termed the 'would/should dilemma'. That is, an individual wishes to achieve something but they are unable to so. According to Rogers, this then generates tension within the individual that in turn produces anxiety.

In applying therapy to resolve the would/should dilemma, Rogers recommends that the therapist must have a 'congruent' or genuine interest in the person. This means that empathy is a central concept to the Rogerian model of client-centred therapy. The ideal aim is to lead the person being counselled to their 'inner beautiful self' so that the individual's would/should dilemma can be overcome. Rogers proposes an egalitarian model of practice in which the teacher is not aloof from the learner but 'with' the learner. Empathy is a particularly important aspect of the Rogerian way. The teacher must be there for the student and prepared to be genuine and assertive. According to Rogers, a genuine person can enable the learner to grow and develop.

Effective practice is facilitated upon resolving the would/should dilemma. Rogers considers that this dilemma is the cause of anxiety, which in turn prevents development. Teachers should also direct students to their 'beautiful inner self'. Rogers believes that all individuals are innately good and that it is only the tension that results from a would/should dilemma that makes the individual a less than good person. Through a genuine and empathetic relationship it is postulated that the would/should dilemma will be replaced by an assertive awareness of one's inner goodness. Although there are many applications for this type of therapy, the generalising assumptions that are made within humanism can mean that its application is restricted.

There are limitations with the concept of empowerment. For learners to become empowered, it is important for them to share the values of their teachers. This is not always possible and is outlined in the work of Watson (2004). When the learners do not share the same values as their teachers, it is often difficult to get a sense of empowerment in the way that Rogers would ideally understand the concept.

Experiential learning

Experiential learning means 'learning from experience'. David Kolb popularised the notion of experiential learning following the influence of John Dewey. As experiential learning is based upon learning as a result of experience, it is often contrasted with didactic teaching. Experiential learning is associated

with learning processes that influence the individual. Many academic programmes in the lifelong learning sector are based on experiential learning. As
opposed to reading about abstract concepts, significant parts of programmes
in the lifelong learning sector are associated with practical vocational learning.

David Kolb's experiential learning model contains four elements: 'active
experimentation', 'concrete experience', 'abstract conceptualisation', and
'reflective observation'. According to Kolb, knowledge is gained as a result
of personal and environmental experiences. Kolb emphasises the importance
of particular abilities if experiential learning is to occur. The learner must be:

- able to become actively involved in the learning experience;
- able to reflect on the experience;
- in possession of the skills to reflect on the experience;
- able to use the new ideas gained from the experience.

Experiential learning requires a willingness to enter into the learning
process. Moon (2004) argues that experiential learning is most effective
when it uses a number of processes. There ought to be a 'reflective learning
phase' alongside a phase where learning occurs as a result of reflecting on the
actions that lead to the implementation of experiential learning. Moon (2004)
also emphasises the importance of learning from feedback in order to enrich
experiential learning.

Most educators realise the importance that experience plays within the
learning process. The role of emotion and feelings is important in learning
from experience. What appears to be vital in experiential learning is that the
individual is directly involved within the experience and then able to reflect
on their experiences using analytical skills. This enhances knowledge and enables information to be retained. Dewey emphasised the importance of reflection. Experiential learning and reflective practice may be viewed as being
elements of the same process. Jacobson and Ruddy (2004) develop Kolb's
learning cycle by asking five questions about the learning process. Their
'5 Questions' model is as follows:

- Did you notice?
- Why did that happen?
- Does that happen in life?
- Why does that happen?
- How can you use that?

Although the emphasis is placed upon the learner and their experience,
it is important to note the importance of reflection for experiential learning.
The facilitator is regarded as being particularly important within the process
of experiential learning.

Experiential learning may be associated with 'learning styles'. Gardner (2000) argues that there are different styles of learning. According to Gardner (2000), 'kinaesthetic learners' prefer learning by doing as opposed to having to rely on didactic teaching. Gardner's ideas have been used by Ofsted to emphasise the importance of practical or experiential learning within the lifelong learning sector.

We can be critical of some of the consequences of an interest in experiential learning. The curriculum within the lifelong learning sector has been given a significant reinterpretation. The days of didactic teaching appear to be in the past as a new interpretation of teaching as 'facilitation' has emerged. Petty (2009) refers to the emergence of teachers as 'guides on the side' as opposed to them being 'sages on a stage'. The past days of 'mastery of one's subject' and 'teacher-led sessions' appear to have been replaced by an emphasis on 'facilitating learning'. The indirect consequence of this may lead to students challenging their learning processes in a way that is not helpful. Learning can only occur through compromise. It is not appropriate to claim that didactic teaching has no place within the learning process. This may be the consequence of too much emphasis being placed on the importance of experiential learning.

Students who combine learning styles have an opportunity to get as much from the learning process as possible. They may in turn develop a variety of skills. As opposed to focusing on either experiential learning or didactic teaching, it seems better to emphasise the importance of having a broad range of learning and teaching techniques that are adapted according to the needs of teachers and learners.

References and further reading

Allen, M. and Ainley, P. (2007) *Education Makes You Fick, Innit? What has Gone Wrong in England's Schools, Colleges and Universities, and How to Start Putting it Right.* London: Tufnell Press.

Atkins, L. (2013) From marginal learning to marginal employment? The real impact of 'learning' employability skills, *Power and Education*, 5(1), 28–37.

Audi, R. (1995) *The Cambridge Dictionary of Philosophy.* Cambridge: Cambridge University Press.

Clegg, S., Hudson, A. and Steel, J. (2010) The emperor's new clothes: globalisation and e-learning in higher education, *British Journal of Sociology of Education*, 24(1), 39–53.

Frick, E., Tardini, S. and Cantoni, L. (2013) *White Paper on Lego® Serious Play®.* Lugano: S-PLA/Lifelong Learning Programme. Available at: http://www.s-play.eu/en/news/70-s-play-white-paper-published [accessed 28 September 2013].

Gardner, H. (2000) *Intelligence Reframed: Multiple Intelligences for the 21st Century.* New York: Basic Books.

Gee, J. (2004) *Situated Language and Learning: A Critique of Traditional Schooling.* London: Routledge.

Gee, J. (2005) Semiotic social spaces and affinity spaces: from the Age of Mythology to today's schools, in D. Barton and K. Tusting (eds.) *Beyond Communities of Practice: Language, Power and Social Context*. Cambridge: Cambridge University Press.

Jacobson, M. and Ruddy, M. (2004) *Open to Outcome: A Practical Guide for Facilitating and Teaching Experiential Reflection*. Oklahoma City, OK: Wood 'N' Barnes Publishing.

Jones, R. (1980) Microcomputers: their uses in primary schools, *Cambridge Journal of Education*, 10, 144–53.

Jones-Thompson, M. (2001) The 'X' in what's next, *The Industry Standard*, 22(4), 80–1.

Moon, J. (2004) *A Handbook of Reflective and Experiential Learning*. London: Routledge.

Petty, G. (2009) *Teaching Today* (4th edn.). Cheltenham: Nelson Thornes.

Selwyn, N. (2011) The place of technology in the Conservative-Liberal Democrat education agenda: an ambition of absence?, *Educational Review*, 63(4), 395–408.

Thatcher, M. (1983) Cited in Hansard House of Commons Parliamentary Questions, 29 March 1983. London: Hansard, House of Commons [40/177-82].

Thomas, L. and Jones, R. (2007) *Embedding Employability in the Context of Widening Participation*. York: Higher Education Academy.

Watson, A. (2004) Reconfiguring the public sphere: implications for analyses of educational policy, *British Journal of Educational Studies*, 52(2), 228–48.

F

Family learning
Flexible learning
Formal learning
Functional skills
Further education

Family learning

Family learning is any kind of formal or informal activity based within the family, involving both parents/guardians/carers and children that can lead to learning. However, it is usually used to refer to specific forms of formal educational provision that are designed to promote learning within the family as a way of securing further benefits for the children of the family as they go through the school curriculum. From the point of view of this book, therefore, the relevance of family learning can be seen in those areas of adult education provision that are primarily designed for parents. A range of providers offer family learning programmes, including local education authorities (LEAs), the Workers' Educational Association (WEA), schools, theatres, and museums. While the scale and nature of family learning provision varies across different providers, a small number of common themes can be discerned:

- The provision of family learning programmes rests on the idea that families are places of learning and that children from families that are not 'learning families' are disadvantaged at school.
- Encouraging parents to participate in family learning can lead to beneficial outcomes for children, who can, for example, receive help from their parents with their homework.
- Family learning can also help so-called 'hard-to-reach' adults who might otherwise be disengaged from lifelong learning, and therefore provide a vehicle for adults who need to reskill or upskill in order to re-enter the job market, for example.

Consequently, some family learning programmes are designed for both parents and children to attend together, while others are designed solely for parents. Typical examples of these kinds of programme include:

Story sacks courses. A story sack is a sack that contains a book (usually a picture book, as story sacks are intended for use with younger children) together with a number of hand-made objects that pertain to the story. Story sacks courses, therefore, can be seen as achieving a number of different things. The courses themselves (which tend to be run by LEAs or volunteer groups working with schools) bring parents together in a learning environment. If the course is accredited, the parents will receive formal recognition of their learning (which may in turn serve as a stimulus to participate in future courses). Once the story sack is complete, the parents will have a rich resource to use with their children, to support their developing listening and language skills.

Literacy and numeracy courses. Alongside 'mainstream' provision of literacy and numeracy classes for adults, many further education colleges and LEAs run courses in outreach centres or in schools for parents designed so that they can in turn help their children with their homework. Courses such as these are particularly effective in encouraging participation from adults who would not otherwise attend; indeed, it is often as a consequence of not being able to help a child with their homework when requested that a parent then chooses to seek out a family learning programme.

Learning programmes centred around 'soft' skills. Galleries and museums (which work towards the same national occupational standards for engaging families in learning as do educational institutions) increasingly offer more-or-less structured resources and activities for family learning ranging from offering simple activity sheets or treasure trails to visitors, to more structured 'family days' that incorporate a range of activities facilitated by appropriately qualified members of staff or volunteers. Activities such as these can sometimes support children's learning at school (depending on the content of the activity) but can also, more importantly, promote participation in learning more generally amongst parents and carers.

Flexible learning

Flexible learning is an example of non-traditional learning. As opposed to being taught in a lifelong learning context, through the week and through the academic year, flexible learning is characterised by learners not being taught conventionally by the teaching staff. For example, the learners may be expected to work on tasks outside the classroom environment. Another example of flexible learning is teaching groups of students together as opposed to teaching the groups individually. The ideal of flexible learning is that the teachers and the learners are as innovative as possible with the curriculum.

The ethos of flexible learning goes against traditional understandings that the curriculum is somehow fixed and rigid. This traditional interpretation of the curriculum results in an expectation that the learners are expected to adapt to the needs of the curriculum. In contrast, flexible learning is based on the idea that the curriculum should be tailored to the needs of individual learners.

There are a variety of reasons why flexible learning is present within the lifelong learning sector. These include pedagogical reasons that have encouraged new interpretations of the curriculum. The curriculum can be brought to life if we think about new ways of learning and teaching (Petty, 2009). Flexible learning can also appeal to the diverse range of learners who are included within the lifelong learning sector. Many people who go into the lifelong learning sector have come from non-traditional learning backgrounds. This may mean that these learners find it difficult to learn in a way that is understood as being conventional. Flexible learning may appeal to the learning needs of these particular learners.

An example of this innovative learning and teaching can be seen in the work of Bers (2008). Since 1994, Marina Bers has conducted research into diverse technological tools ranging from robotics to virtual worlds. A central theme within Bers' research is the use of technology within the classroom. Bers has explored how learners can use robotic manipulatives to explore concepts in an innovative way. A specific example of this approach is exemplified by Bers' (2010) work on how 'citizenship' values can be developed through technology. These citizenship values are described by Bers as 'assets' and 'behaviours'. Desirable assets such as being 'caring' and 'confident' are characterised by forms of behaviour that include 'effective communication skills' and 'creativity'. Bers (2008) has attempted to develop these attributes in learners through creating a virtual 'school of the future'. In this virtual world, the learners are required to create an 'ideal school environment' that is characterised by collaboration and harmony.

Sometimes flexible learning is introduced for the wrong reasons. For example, the motive for flexible learning may have more to do with finance; groups may be combined together and contact may be reduced if there are not enough teachers. This is an example of flexible learning being used for reasons other than helping everyone benefit from the curriculum. There might also be an appeal to flexible learning as a direct result of the pressures experienced by individuals teaching and learning in the lifelong learning sector. It is thus important to ensure that the motive for this form of learning is the wish to be innovative about the curriculum, and nothing else.

Formal learning

Formal learning is the term used to refer to any process of learning that takes place in a formal context, in the context of a formal curriculum. It is important to recognise that the notion of 'formal' learning does not imply that the process of learning in a structured environment is in any way different to the kind of learning that takes place informally. However learning might be defined or understood (as a behavioural process, on the one hand, or as a consequence of participation in a *community of practice*, on the other), it is the same across both formal *and* informal contexts.

The further education and lifelong learning sector is characterised in part by variety. Further education colleges vary – sometimes considerably – in size, in character, and in terms of the curricula that they offer, and the student groups that they attract. And this variety is reflected in the nature of the student population. In turn, lifelong learning provision is more diverse. Adult education courses take place in community centres, public libraries, function rooms above pubs. Adult learners come from a variety of social backgrounds, and study a wider range of courses. There are many different awarding bodies offering many different qualifications in the sector. But all such provision can be classified in terms of formal provision.

The characteristic elements of formal learning provision can therefore be understood, in the first instance, in terms of the formal *curriculum* that is being followed. The curriculum documentation acts to define:

- the body of skills or knowledge – the course content – that will be studied;
- the ways in which students' learning will be assessed, and how feedback will be provided;
- the resources (e.g. books, materials, staff, buildings) that will minimally be required;
- the ways in which its delivery will be evaluated for quality assurance purposes.

The provision of structures such as these, within which teaching and learning occur, mark out the process as being a formal one, the pedagogical activities chosen by the teacher notwithstanding, the qualitative nature of the teaching environment, and the nature of the assessment process. Thus, although an AAT class for accounting technicians might at first seem to be 'more formal' than a counselling course accredited by NCFE, and a City & Guilds Certificate in electrical installation might seem 'more formal' than an ESOL class – in both cases due to the styles of activities and assessments employed during the programmes in question – they are all examples of accredited provision that therefore provide opportunities for formal, not informal, learning.

The concept of formal learning should be understood clearly in a positive sense, in contrast to the negative views sometimes held. Lecturing in 'a formal style', for example, is often perceived as involving rows of silent students listening to a lecturer reading from their notes, delivering that element of the course in a didactic manner. Instead, formal learning, in the sense in which it is used here, is intended to refer to an approach to learning – and by extension to planning for learning – that is characterised by the structures and processes of education systems that have developed in the UK since the nineteenth century, and more specifically during the last 60 years. Therefore, the 'formal learning' that is provided in further education colleges and adult education centres requires (but need not be restricted to) institutions, staff, curricula, programmes, classrooms, and virtual learning environments.

Functional skills

Functional skills refer to those skills required in English, maths, and ICT (information and communications technologies). These skills are regarded as being particularly important for the lifelong learning sector. The relationship between 'employability' and the lifelong learning sector has led to an emphasis on providing programmes of study that equip learners with the skills necessary for employment. Functional skills are considered to be an update on the previous notion of 'key skills'. A 3-year pilot of functional skills ended in 2010. Level 1 and 2 functional skills are to be examined at the lifelong learning centre and then assessed and moderated externally. The assessments are not embedded within other subjects. This makes functional skills different to key skills. The pass or fail elements are determined by external assessments. Functional Skills Mathematics is based on mathematical problem solving and decision making using numbers. Functional Skills English is based on speaking, listening, and communication, together with reading and writing that tests spelling and grammar. Functional Skills ICT is based on problem solving using all forms of ICT.

The emergence of functional skills is relevant for the debate on whether the curriculum within the lifelong learning sector should be for academic development in itself or used to address an employability agenda. Academics (including Lucas, 2007) have commented on the problems that can result from an employability agenda – an emphasis emerges on what is referred to by Urban (2008) as the 'end product'. Accordingly, the curriculum within the lifelong learning sector has been influenced by this agenda. Instead of focusing upon educational processes, the employability agenda sees the final goal or final destination as the most important element. The implication of the employability agenda is that English, maths and ICT become a central part of the curriculum of the lifelong learning sector.

Another criticism of functional skills is the claim that they are 'a return to the past'. The Coalition government in the UK appears to favour a return to 'traditional educational values', including 'testing' and 'the 3 Rs' – reading, writing, and arithmetic. Critics of the employability agenda (Harris and Islar, 2013; Mayo, 2013) highlight how unfair a curriculum is that generates 'winners' and 'losers'. In the UK, it is politicians who drive the functional skills agenda, as they want to ensure that the country is able to compete with the emerging economies of India and China. A merit of this critique of functional skills is that attention is drawn to the oppressive nature of the employability agenda. Education is about realising individual potential in its fullest sense. Unless this notion of education is propagated, we may continue to do what Coffield (2006) sees as 'running ever faster down the wrong road'.

Further education

Ingleby and Hunt (2008) view further education as being characterised by a range of educational institutions offering an even more varied range of educational programmes. Further education (the precursor to the lifelong learning sector) is characterised by diversity, with complex educational challenges presenting a range of fascinating issues for teachers and learners to consider. As Geertz (1988: 2) has phrased it, it can be 'Heraclitus cubed and worse'! The state of flux that has been popularised by the philosopher Heraclitus is made manifest within the institutions that make up further education. There are large-scale 'mixed-economy' institutions offering 'higher education' and 'further education'. Alongside these are smaller scale institutions offering either 'higher education' or 'further education'. Many of these educational institutions have their origins in the post-war educational expansion of the 1950s and 1960s. Up until 2010, many colleges were affected by New Labour's Private Finance Initiative of building new or refurbished lifelong learning centres.

The learners associated with further education are also characterised by diversity. They include school pupils studying vocational subjects such as 'health and social care', alongside adults studying for a degree-level qualification (e.g. foundation degree). Moreover, the staff who work in this environment come from a range of backgrounds. There are academics with PhD qualifications, teachers with qualified teacher status (QTS), and lecturers with vocational backgrounds in areas such as 'painting and decorating' who may not have any formal teaching qualifications.

The further education sector is now known as the lifelong learning sector. Any organisation or sector that changes its name usually does so for a good reason. The further education sector was referred to colloquially as being 'the Cinderella' of the English education system. The implication is that 'further education 'did not receive adequate investment and that it was neglected compared with primary and secondary education. As a result of this perception, the sector is now referred to as the lifelong learning sector. The advantages to teaching and learning in the sector were based on the variety of programmes available to non-traditional learners. Many of the traditional students in the colleges were individuals who were not academic and left school to study for non-vocational qualifications. There was also an ethos in many colleges of 'serving the community'. A further education college was there to serve the needs of the local community. This meant that many of the colleges had a clear vision of what they were expected to do.

Further education experienced a transformation under the Conservative governments of 1979–1997. A new vision of 'incorporation' was introduced that generated a 'market', as colleges were expected to manage budgets and compete with other colleges for students. This appeared to be the end of the ethos of community spirit that characterised many colleges. Competition, financial pressure and the introduction of Ofsted as an inspection regime appeared to combine to produce the new vision of a lifelong learning sector. With the new name there appears to be a wish to have a stable sector of education that is equal to primary and secondary education in attempting to produce the best educational standards for as long as possible throughout the life course.

References and further reading

Bers, M. (2008) *Blocks to Robots: Learning with Technology in the Early Childhood Classroom.* New York: Teachers College Press.

Bers, M. (2010) *Virtual worlds as playgrounds for learning.* Paper presented at the International Virtual Environments Research Group Conference, 28–29 June, Teesside University, Middlesbrough.

Coffield, F. (2006) *Running ever faster down the wrong road.* Inaugural Lecture, University of London Institute of Education, London.

Geertz, C. (1988) *Works and Lives: The Anthropologist as Author.* Stanford, CA: Stanford University Press.

Harris, L. and Islar, M. (2013) Neoliberalism, nature and changing modalities of environmental governance in contemporary Turkey, in Y. Atasoy (ed.) *Global Economic Crisis and the Politics of Diversity.* London: Palgrave Macmillan.

Ingleby, E. and Hunt, J. (2008) The CPD needs of mentors in post-compulsory initial teacher training in England, *Journal of In-Service Education,* 34(1), 61–75.

Lucas, N. (2007) The in-service training of adult literacy, numeracy and English for Speakers of Other Languages teachers in England: the challenges of a 'standards-led model', *Journal of In-Service Education,* 33(1), 125–42.

Mayo, P. (2013) *Echoes from Freire for a Critically Engaged Pedagogy.* London: Bloomsbury.

Petty, G. (2009) *Teaching Today* (4th edn.). Cheltenham: Nelson Thornes.

Urban, M. (2008) Dealing with uncertainty: challenges and possibilities for the early childhood profession, *European Early Childhood Education Research Journal,* 16(2), 135–52.

G

Gender

Gender

Gender in the lifelong learning sector refers to the influence that biological identity has in influencing educational performance. There is interest in whether an individual's gender has an impact upon educational achievement. Some areas in the lifelong sector have been especially influenced by gender (for example, early years programmes appear to attract significant numbers of females as staff and students). The gender balance of both students and staff confirms what Parker-Rees *et al.* (2004: 128) refer to as 'the overwhelmingly female' children's workforce in the UK and beyond.

The children's workforce being educated in the lifelong learning sector in the UK might initially appear to be quite homogeneous, as opposed to being characterised by competing professional stakeholders. Ninety-nine per cent of the children's workforce in the UK are female (DCSE, 2003), so gender is a key factor that shapes interaction within this context. McKie *et al.* (2001: 233) claim that gender is important because women are treated differently in the labour market in general. Simpson (2011: 700), however, argues that gender does not fully explain differences in pay and status within the children's workforce because this educational context is more diverse than it might initially appear. This is a result of the divisions in pay and status between female workers who are working within different educational roles within the children's workforce. Moreover, Osgood (2005: 209) identifies that 'the vast majority of childcare workers are working class' and argues that gender and social class become 'intertwined issues'. This is a further way of revealing the complexity of how gender impacts upon this educational context.

Becoming aware of gender issues within the lifelong learning sector may result in teaching and learning activities becoming as inclusive as possible. Programmes that appear to be dominated by one gender at the expense of another may need to be promoted positively to the other sex. For example, early years programmes should be promoted to males so that they enrol as students on these programmes. Other vocational areas (e.g. engineering) need to be promoted to females so that these are not monopolised by males. The extent to which education can make a difference also needs to be considered. Interpretations of what one biological sex can or cannot do are entrenched in wider social factors. The complexity of these socio-economic issues means that that it is difficult to initiate change. We must recognise that there is only so much that can be achieved within the lifelong learning sector.

It is important to ensure that stereotypes of what individuals can and cannot do are not reinforced within the learning sector. The assumption that all male learners enjoy practical activities and all female learners enjoy learning with books is a negative stereotype that should not be reinforced. Learning activities ought to be made as inclusive as possible so that as broad a curriculum as possible is provided. This way of providing as inclusive a curriculum as possible may be regarded as one way of dealing with gender issues. Instead of assuming that particular learners can achieve particular targets based on gender, it is better to include as many learners as possible regardless of their gender.

There is interest in gender within academic subject areas, including sociology and philosophy. There is interest in how the interpretation of biology is used within educational contexts. Biology is understood as being 'open to interpretation' as opposed to being fixed. The dominance of a particular gender is a consequence of power regimes and discourse. Depending upon the theoretical approach adopted, this expression of power is a product of socio-economic factors and interpretation. The consequences are regarded as being social as opposed to being fixed and determined by biology.

References and further reading

Department for Children, Schools and Families (DCSF) (2003) *Every Child Matters.* Norwich: The Stationery Office.

McKie, L., Bowlby, S. and Gregory, S. (2001) Gender, caring and employment in Britain, *Journal of Social Policy*, 30(2), 233–58.

Osgood, J. (2005) Who cares? The classed nature of childcare, *Gender and Education*, 17(3), 289–303.

Parker-Rees, R., Leeson, C., Willan, J. and Savage, J. (2004) *Early Childhood Studies.* Exeter: Learning Matters.

Simpson, D. (2011) Reform, inequalities of process and the transformative potential of communities of practice in the pre-school sector in England, *British Journal of Sociology of Education*, 32(5), 699–716.

H

Higher education
Human capital

Higher education

The UK higher education sector is a significant contributor to lifelong learning provision, historically through the provision of extension or extra-mural classes, more recently through the expansion of part-time degree provision, and at the time of writing through new forms of curricular provision that draws on new technologies (such as MOOCs – massive open online courses). While the vast majority of higher education courses continue to cater for the 'typical' university student (leaving school with three A-levels or equivalent), a significant proportion of provision is directed towards part-time students, adults who may be returning to study after raising a family or after deciding to change career. For these students, higher education might represent a 'second chance', a route to a new job or a personal ambition. Within higher education, such provision is commonly clumped together under the heading 'non-traditional'. This is a somewhat imperfect label, implying as it does that there is something novel or awkward about part-time provision for adult returners; in fact, UK universities have a long history of offering such provision, although it has changed significantly in character over time, especially in the last 20 years or so, as the provision of recreational learning opportunities has dwindled.

It is through the provision of part-time courses that the higher education sector contributes significantly to lifelong learning. And the numbers of students involved are significant: in the academic year 2011–2012, almost half a million part-time students (almost two-thirds of whom were female) were enrolled onto a variety of certificate, diploma and degree courses at different universities. Some universities have significant numbers of part-time students. Discounting the Open University, which is something of a special case as it was founded specifically to provide part-time university education for distance learners, a number of other universities (both new and old) have large numbers of part-time students, including Birkbeck College, University of London (almost all of Birkbeck's students are part time), Teesside University in the Tees Valley (where, at the time of writing, part-time students outnumber full-time students by two to one), and the University of Hull (with a population of over 7000 part-time students in contrast to a full-time population of 21,000). Part-time students follow courses that are delivered in a variety of modes, including both 'traditional' face-to-face provision, usually in the evening or at weekends (although some universities also offer intensive week-long programmes), and distance learning provision, increasingly through the use of virtual learning environments. While the broad higher education curriculum is available to part-time students, a significant majority (over one-third) focus on a relatively small number of areas: healthcare-related; education; and business and administration.

Just as changes to government policy and funding regimes led to the collapse of much 'recreational' adult education provision at universities in the early 1990s, so more recent changes to university funding arrangements have impacted on part-time provision. The introduction of fees for full-time students gained considerable media coverage. Changes to part-time funding were less extensively reported, and while the facility for part-time students to access loans to cover fee payments is to be partially welcomed (loans are only available for students who are new to higher education, not to those who are retraining or gaining postgraduate professional qualifications), the reduction in other sources of direct government funding aimed at widening access raises the possibility of a further decline in part-time student numbers. Over the period 2002–2012, full-time student numbers increased by 17 per cent (remembering that the Labour government's ambition for 50 per cent of the population to have access to higher education was quietly shelved), while part-time student numbers fell by 11 per cent. It is to be hoped that this decline can be arrested if the 'second chances' offered by lifelong learning departments at UK universities are to be sustained.

Human capital

Human capital is associated with the work of the French philosopher Pierre Bourdieu. Bourdieu's (1986, 1993) work can be used to explain the differing interpretations of the lifelong learning sector. There are competing stakeholders in education who are attempting to gain capital at the expense of others. For Bourdieu, education is part of the process of 'cultural reproduction', as the role of the education system is to replicate the values of the dominant social classes. The conversations about education either perpetuate the existing educational order or, conversely, promote new understandings of the purpose of education. Bourdieu (1986: 62) refers to the potentially volatile nature of education, with its 'profits' and 'sanctions', when he writes:

> Every linguistic situation functions as a market on which the speaker places his products, and the product he produces for this market depends on his anticipation of the price his products will receive. We enter the educational market with an expectation of the profits and sanctions we shall receive.

Bourdieu is arguing here that although shared understandings of teaching and learning perpetuate the educational field, there is also the presence of conflict in the realm of ideas about education. Bourdieu (1993) has popularised the notion of 'cultural capital' by claiming that a main purpose of the education system is to facilitate this 'cultural reproduction'. According to him:

> In every epoch there is a constant struggle over the rate of exchange between the different kinds of capital, a struggle among the different fractions of the dominant class, whose overall capital is composed in differing proportions of the various kinds of capital. (Bourdieu, 1986: 34)

The 'constant struggle' within the educational context is a consequence of the inherent contradictions that operate within unequal societies. These inherent contradictions hold the potential to produce competing ideologies that hold different understandings of the purpose of education.

Bourdieu's work has been applied by a number of educational researchers (e.g. Ingleby and Tummons, 2012) in analysing the dynamics of the lifelong learning sector. Part of the appeal of Bourdieu's work on human capital is that it explains creativity within set economic frameworks. Although the same economic structures are in place, there are varying interpretations of these structures by human beings engaging with them. The rapidly changing nature of the lifelong learning sector can be understood according to this philosophical framework. Students, teachers and everyone else associated with the lifelong learning sector are engaging in a process of trying to maximise as much capital as possible in order to do as well as they can. Critics of Bourdieu (for example, traditional Marxist thinkers) argue that the emphasis on human capital lessens the importance of fundamental economic structures. Instead of focusing on individual human agents, the recommendation is to study the underlying economic causes that shape human behaviour.

The work of Bourdieu (1986, 1993) can be applied to understand the neoliberal marketisation of education in the lifelong learning sector. Bourdieu (1986: 62) draws attention to the competition that can exist between educational stakeholders as they compete for the 'profits' of the 'educational market'. Moreover, this notion of competing stakeholders helps make clear why the key ingredients of Wenger's (1998) understanding of a community of practice appear to be subsumed within many current recommendations for best practice in the lifelong learning sector. The goal of having a 'shared domain of interest' has emerged as a key strategy in neoliberal policy initiatives in general. This aspect of workforce reform appears to be recommended as an antidote to the fragmentation that may result from competing stakeholders as they struggle to acquire educational capital.

References and further reading

Bourdieu, P. (1986) *Questions de sociologie*. Paris: Les Editions de Minuit.

Bourdieu, P. (1993) *Outline of a Theory of Practice*. Cambridge: Cambridge University Press.

Ingleby, E. and Tummons, J. (2012) Repositioning professionalism: teachers, mentors, policy and praxis, *Research in Post-Compulsory Education*, 17(2), 163–79.

Wenger, E. (1998) *Communities of Practice*. Cambridge: Cambridge University Press.

I

Inclusion
Informal learning
Institute for Learning
IQER

Inclusion

Tomlinson (1997) defines inclusion as the greatest degree of match or fit between how learners learn best, what they need and want to learn, and what is required of the sector, a college and teachers for successful learning to take place. For Tummons (2009: 94), 'inclusive practice' is: 'thinking about our teaching, and our curricula, in such a way that any student can access it to the best of their potential ability'. Petty (2009) discusses differentiation along similar lines and defines it as adopting strategies that ensure success in learning for all, by accommodating individual differences of any kind. This interest in inclusive learning is based on a fundamental theme that in order to provide the best opportunities for learning to take place, we must be flexible and adapt our teaching practices accordingly. In summary, 'inclusion' can be defined as: the use of a variety of differentiated approaches to teaching and learning in the classroom in order to deliver the curriculum content in such a way as to promote the widest possible access to learning for as many learners as possible.

If we consider the previous definitions of inclusion and think further about the implications for curriculum development, a key related area for consideration is differentiation. You will often find inclusion and differentiation discussed together because inclusive learning links to differentiated teaching and learning practices. So what is a differentiated classroom? Tomlinson (2001: 1) describes a differentiated classroom as one that 'provides different avenues to acquiring content, to processing or making sense of ideas and to developing products so that each student can learn effectively'. Tomlinson

(1997) then goes on to discuss the advantages of a differentiated classroom: it provides the best access to learning, promotes effectiveness of learning, and encourages motivation in learning. Tomlinson's (1997) notion of a differentiated classroom emphasises that learning experiences need to be based upon readiness to learn, learning interests and learning profiles. The content and activities in the session and the expected learning outcomes are developed according to the varied needs of the group and the individual learners. The consequences are that teaching and learning activities are focused on key concepts of learning so that teachers and students work together to ensure that learners are challenged and continually engaged in learning. Some of Tomlinson's (1997) teaching and learning strategies to promote a differentiated learning experience for the learners can be summarised as follows:

- The teacher should combine time and space with effective learning activities.
- Flexible grouping is required to ensure fluidity of working arrangements that are consistent as far as possible.
- This should include a range of strategies such as whole-class learning, paired learning, small group learning, teacher-selected learning groups and random learning groups.
- Flexible use of time is needed to respond to the learners' needs at any given time.
- A wide variety of classroom management strategies are needed such as independent study, interest groups, learning buddies and tiered assignments in order to help to target instruction to the students' needs.

There should be clear criteria for success developed at both group and individual level to provide guidance to the children as to what would be a successful learning outcome. Formative and summative assessment activities should be varied to enable the learners to demonstrate their own thoughts and develop their learning. These broader but important factors provide some theoretical parameters to guide the more practical aspects of planning for teaching and learning. This means that developing schemes of work and planning delivery are critical aspects of the curriculum process.

Informal learning

Informal learning is the term used to refer to any process of learning that takes place in an informal context, in the absence of any formal curriculum. It is important to recognise that the notion of 'informal' learning does not imply that the process of learning in an unstructured environment is in any way different to the kind of learning that takes place as a consequence of enrolling as a student on a formal programme of study. However learning might be defined or understood (as a behavioural process, on the one hand, or as a consequence of participation in a *community of practice*, on the other), it is the same across both informal *and* formal contexts.

Informal learning can be either planned or unplanned. That is, any episode of informal learning might emerge from a conscious desire to practise or acquire a new body of skills or knowledge, such as wanting to learn how to list items for sale on a website and sitting down in front of a desktop computer with the express intent of 'teaching oneself' how to do so. Or an episode might emerge in a more implicit and less organised manner, such as through trial and error when using a new smartphone for the first time.

Informal learning can require the individual to act as an 'auto-didact', a person who teaches themselves about a particular topic through self-study, perhaps by borrowing non-fiction books from a local library or reading material online. It can also involve other people while still remaining informal. A new smartphone user or online trader might ask a friend how to complete a particular task such as accessing a wi-fi hotspot or opening an account to manage online payments. As such, informal learning can always be seen as involving other people, as never being a solitary process. Whether it is through talking with others and asking them for help, reading a book or accessing a website, other people are always involved – to varying degrees – in the informal learning of an individual or group of people. At one level, therefore, it can be argued that informal learning can – although this is by no means essential – involve some form of intended instruction. The person who demonstrates the accessing of a wi-fi hotspot is teaching their friend how to do something, although no formal pedagogic structures are present. The author of a non-fiction book writes with the express intention of capturing a particular series of issues, arguments or perspectives within the book's pages, so that they can be read and perhaps change people's opinions or attitudes. The author of the 'teach yourself' book is more overt in their intention to provide a pedagogic context. All of these are examples of an intention to teach something to somebody, although they sit entirely outside formal educational structures. These are examples of informal learning, but with some element of formal instruction intended.

The relevance and importance of informal learning processes such as these – particularly within the further education and lifelong learning sector – is to be found in the practice of the *accreditation of prior learning* (APL). APL acknowledges that the kinds of learning that happen in everyday life are of legitimate value and can be used to allow access to opportunities for *formal learning* as well as for the certification or accreditation of learning that might have taken place in an informal setting, but which – if properly recognised – might be used to gain formal qualifications.

Institute for Learning

The Institute for Learning (IfL) is the professional body for teachers, assessors, and trainers in the further and adult education sectors (including community education, offender learning, and work-based learning). It was originally established in 2002 on a voluntary paying basis, but gained prominence following the decision in 2007 to make membership of the Institute compulsory for all teachers and trainers in the sector. This decision accompanied the wider professional reforms affecting the lifelong learning sector that were undertaken by the then Labour government, including the requirements for all new teachers to work towards a teaching qualification and the establishment of a new body of professional standards under the purview of (the now defunct) Lifelong Learning UK.

The period from 2007 to 2012 was a busy time for the IfL. As well as seeing a rise in (compulsory) membership, the Institute was also chosen (although there cannot have been any serious competition) as the body that would manage two linked processes. The first of these was the auditing of continuing professional development (CPD) for teachers in the lifelong learning sector, which was to be made compulsory for the first time, in line with many other professions. Full-time teachers would be expected to complete 30 hours of CPD (pro-rata for part-time staff). The definition of CPD chosen by the IfL was generous, and included a variety of informal as well as formal activities. Linked to this was the process of professional formation, a sequence of post-qualification (that is, to be carried out after the completion of a CertEd/ PGCE or equivalent) development activities that would lead to the award of a new professional status: qualified teacher, learning and skills (QTLS). The introduction of QTLS was seen as an important first step in establishing professional parity with schoolteachers holding QTS (qualified teacher status).

The Wolf Report (2011) recommended to the Coalition government that schools should be able to employ teachers with QTLS, a recommendation that was immediately enacted by the Secretary of State for Education, Michael Gove. However, during 2012 and 2013, a series of further reforms have, arguably, rendered this concession somewhat redundant. In 2012, government financial support for the IfL was withdrawn, the requirement for staff to register with the IfL was repealed, and professional formation leading to QTLS status was made voluntary. Moreover, routes to gaining employment in a secondary school have changed. Whereas the IfL positioned QTLS status as a 'passport' to the secondary sector, a position implicitly endorsed by the Wolf Report, the move to change secondary schools into academies – which are not obliged to employ teaching staff with either professional qualifications or professional licenses – has made this need for QTLS redundant. If, as the current (in 2013) government indicates, the majority of secondary schools will become academies, the incentive for QTLS will recede further. With the

IfL setting a fee for professional formation of £485 in February 2013, it is likely that demand for this process will decrease in the current (at the time of writing) atmosphere of voluntarism.

Other contentious issues related to the work of the IfL have included: claims that the leadership was too remote from the membership; disagreements between the IfL and the University and College Union (UCU) over fees; and intervention from the Association of Colleges (AoC) regarding disciplinary measures against staff for non-payment of IfL membership fees during the period of compulsory membership.

IQER

IQER refers to the Intergrated Quality Enhancement Review that has become associated with the lifelong learning sector. IQER is a review method specifically devised for higher education in further education colleges in England. It replaced the 'Academic Review of Subjects', which operated for the last time in 2006–2007. IQER is normally in two parts: (1) a developmental engagement where the QAA (Quality Assurance Agency) works collaboratively with the college; and (2) a more formal summative review that results in a published report on the QAA website.

The review process is characterised by a series of visits to the higher education institutions. A lead university may be involved in a number of higher education business partnerships (HEBPs). The IQER process is responsible for assessing the quality of educational provision that is provided by the programme. An example of a recent IQER process occurred with a degree programme delivered by five college centres. The academic programme is coordinated by a lead higher education institution which is responsible for the academic curriculum. The academic programme is based on sociological, psychological, pedagogical, and social policy content. Each of the first year modules introduces content that is reinforced by the modules that are studied in the second year of the programme. The programme is assessed via a combination of essays, reports, case-study reflections, and portfolio reflections. The IQER process visited each of the college centres once a year for three years in order to assess the quality of the academic programme. At the end of the three years, a report was disseminated that commented upon good practice as well as making developmental recommendations for how the programme could be improved.

The role that IQER has in ensuring standards of high-quality teaching and learning is debatable. For example, can a week's visit once a year for three years help to improve standards of teaching and learning? There is also concern over the methodology that is applied by IQER. Like Ofsted, much of the process appears to be based upon the 'inspection visit'. It is difficult to assess the effectiveness of this process of audit. The emphasis that is placed upon the college centre running the degree is another complicated aspect of the IQER process. The lead university has limited involvement in the IQER process, yet this institution is effectively responsible for the academic curriculum. The programme content, its assessments, and module content are likely to have been written by this higher education institution. There are also concerns about the ambiguity of the IQER process. The developmental recommendations can appear vague and it is difficult to know if they are being implemented. Moreover, IQER appears to be something of a reaction against Ofsted. The 'softly, softly' process adopted by IQER almost appears to be an acceptance that the Ofsted system is not right!

The 'tension' and 'conflict' that is associated with IQER links again to the ideas of Jürgen Habermas (1989). The tension within the audit process links to the Habermasian understanding of the nature of 'advanced capitalist societies'. Habermas argues that modern capitalist societies such as the UK are subject to crises within the realm of ideas. The tension that appears to exist between the teaching profession and IQER is a further example of this 'tension in the realm of ideas'. A further consideration regarding IQER is that it is yet another example of a process of audit that is being applied to the lifelong learning sector. The number of inspections and the range of processes of audit do not in any way ensure best practice will result. Perhaps it would be better to focus on the curriculum and its development as opposed to focusing on the audit process?

References and further reading

Habermas, J. (1989) *The Structural Transformation of the Public Sphere: An Inquiry into Bourgeois Society.* Cambridge, MA: MIT Press.

Petty, G. (2009) *Teaching Today* (4th edn.). Cheltenham: Nelson Thornes.

Powell, S. and Tummons, J. (2010) *Inclusive Practice in the Lifelong Learning Sector.* Exeter: Learning Matters.

Tomlinson, C.A. (1997) *Differentiation of Instruction in Mixed Ability Classrooms.* Boise, ID: Idaho Council for Exceptional Children.

Tomlinson, C. (2001) *How to Differentiate in Mixed Ability Classrooms.* London: Association for Supervision and Curriculum Development.

Tummons, J. (2009) *Curriculum Studies in the Lifelong Learning Sector.* Exeter: Learning Matters.

Tummons, J. (2011) *Curriculum Studies in the Lifelong Learning Sector* (2nd edn.). Exeter: Learning Matters.

Wolf, A. (2011) *Review of Vocational Education* (The Wolf Report). London: Department for Education/Department for Business, Innovation and Skills.

J

Jargon

The term 'jargon' simply refers to the use of particular words or expressions by specific individuals or groups. It is usually used to refer to the ways in which professional groups such as lawyers or architects speak – but it is a term that is equally applicable to other groups, whether they are cycle mechanics discussing the new components to be fitted onto a bicycle frame or hobbyists discussing their shared interests. It is often used in a disparaging manner to criticise the ways in which particular people talk or particular documents are written, although the term need not in itself carry negative connotations.

There is a lot of jargon in further education and lifelong learning: 'learning styles', 'quality assurance' and 'differentiation' to name three (which, not entirely coincidentally, are included within this book). And there are many acronyms in use as well ('SfL – Skills for Life'; 'GLH – Guided Learning Hours'). Over recent years, both individuals and organisations have been concerned that the use of jargon leads to confusion at best and disempowerment at worst. The Plain English Campaign (founded in 1979) is the best-known example of such an organisation, and there has also been an increase in academic interest in how jargon is used. Mindful of the problems – and criticisms – that surround the use of jargon, the provision of a glossary or 'jargon buster' has become increasingly commonplace in official publications, both in print and online. Curriculum documents from awarding bodies such as City & Guilds or Edexcel often contain glossaries and further education colleges often have jargon busters on their websites.

As the use of jargon is a common feature of working practice in the lifelong learning sector, it does not follow that it – or any other body of specialist language – need always be problematic. Any community of people who are engaged in a shared series of activities or practices will develop its own language use over time, and people who are outside the community will not always easily understand this. Many people working within further and adult education (as well as other education sectors) know what 'quality assurance', 'differentiation', and 'learning styles' are – and this is knowledge that will have been acquired during the course of professional development (while studying for a CertEd/PGCE, for example) or derived from experience in the workplace. Terms such as these are undoubtedly examples of jargon, but they are simply expressions that capture particular aspects of, and ideas that belong to, the lifelong learning sector as a place where people work. That is, they are simply examples of the words or phrases that are used by particular speech communities (Swales, 1990). When people – new students or new trainee teachers, for example – first encounter these and other terms, they do not and should not automatically cause difficulties. They simply need to be properly defined and explored, in such a way that their meanings are established, and that the debates and disagreements around these meanings are highlighted. Concerns regarding the excessive use of jargon should always be heeded, but it is important not to confuse the use of jargon with a poor or deliberately confusing style of writing. It is perfectly possible to produce a piece of writing without jargon that is confusing to the reader, or to produce a piece of writing that is clear and easy to follow that uses jargon that is necessary and appropriate for the intended readership of the piece.

References and further reading

Gee, J. (1996) *Social Linguistics and Literacies: Ideology in Discourses* (2nd edn.). London: Routledge Falmer.
Swales, J. (1990) *Genre Analysis: English in Academic and Research Settings.* Cambridge: Cambridge University Press.

K

Key skills
Knowledge

Key skills

The lifelong learning sector has been influenced in its development by the changes within the English university system. There has been a move away from an elite, publicly funded system paying the fees of a minority of students. Whereas only 5 per cent of the school-leaving population went to university in the 1960s, this elite, publicly funded mode of English university education has been transformed to currently include 45 per cent of school leavers (Brennan *et al.*, 2010). As well as this demographic change within English universities, there has been an evolution of the academic curriculum of the UK. Vocational professions that include nursing, social work and the academic curriculum featured in this research (early childhood studies) have joined the traditional professions of medicine, the law and education (and their associated academic degrees). This transformation in the curriculum has led to the introduction of skills that lead to employability (or key skills). Courses of study that result in employment are in turn promoted as being the most worthwhile programmes.

Key skills are understood to be maths, English and ICTs. They are embedded within courses in the lifelong sector in order to enhance the employability potential of students. The predecessor of the lifelong learning sector (the further education sector) existed to provide an alternative to the academic curriculum through its provision of vocational education. The lifelong learning sector is also synonymous with employability and 'standards-led' vocational education. Lucas (2007) draws attention to the implications of 'standards-led education' and its consequences for the curriculum. There appears to have been an emphasis placed upon what is referred to by Urban (2008) as the 'end product'. Instead of a focus on educational processes, the final goal or final destination appears to be the most important element within this employ-ability agenda. The curriculum within the lifelong learning sector has been influenced accordingly by this agenda. Traditionally, students who undertook 'further education' were those students who had not done well in school. It can be argued that part of the appeal of the further education system rested in the difference it offered to the curriculum in the schools. The complication of the employability agenda has witnessed subjects that caused students to leave school becoming part of the lifelong learning sector.

'Core skills' – or 'key skills' (English, maths, and ICTs) – are part of many of the vocational programmes within the lifelong learning sector. It can be argued that this is a consequence of the emphasis that is placed on employ-ability. There are critics of this employability agenda. Archer and Leathwood (2003), Freire (1973, 1985, 1994), Giroux (2000), Harris and Islar (2013), Mayo (2013), Morley and Dunstan (2013), Torres (1998, 2008) and Williams (2013), all criticise the employability agenda on moral grounds. One of their main objections is that the employability agenda evidences oppression and exploi-tation (or 'unfairness'). Authors including Freire (1973, 1985, 1994), Giroux (2000) and Torres (1998) have attempted to place 'moral education' at the centre of educational policies. In contrast, the varying approaches to policy adopted by the politicians are influenced by their political beliefs and eco-nomic priorities. The perceived importance of globalisation and the need to compete with other emerging economies has been identified as a key element of teaching in the lifelong learning sector. Critical pedagogy disputes the rationale behind this approach to teaching for moral reasons. Critical peda-gogy is opposed to the bilateral priorities of economics and politics we see within the employability agenda. There is instead a recommendation for sys-tematic enquiries into teaching and learning in order to develop pedagogy. It is this attempt to create understandings as well as change that lies at the heart of critical pedagogy. A merit of critical pedagogy is that attention is drawn to the oppressive nature of the employability agenda. Education is about realis-ing individual potential in its fullest sense. Unless this notion of education is propagated, we may continue to do what Coffield (2006) sees as 'running ever faster down the wrong road'.

Knowledge

Knowledge is associated with the Greek word *episteme* and the study of know-ledge. Over time, philosophers have identified different types of knowledge. An example is 'propositional knowledge' (or 'that something is so'). A primary concern for philosophy in the seventeenth and eighteenth centuries was the extent of our *a priori* knowledge. Rationalists including Descartes, Leibniz and Spinoza contended that all true knowledge is *a priori*. Empiricists including

Locke, Berkeley and Hume argued that all knowledge is *a posteriori*. In his *Critique of Pure Reason* (1781), Kant reconciled the two ideas.

A posteriori knowledge is now understood to be knowledge that depends upon supporting sensory experiences. *A priori* knowledge, by way of contrast, is understood to be knowledge that has no such dependence. Kant argued that *a priori* knowledge comes from intellectual processes referred to as 'pure reason' or 'pure understanding'. Knowledge of mathematical truths is an example of *a priori* knowledge, while knowledge of physical objects is an example of *a posteriori* knowledge.

Since the time of Plato (400 BC), epistemologists have sought to identify the essential components of knowledge. A traditional view suggested by Plato and Kant is that propositional knowledge (knowledge that something is so) is based on justification, truth, and belief:

- *Justification*: knowledge is not simply true belief. Some true beliefs are supported by guesswork. They do not qualify as knowledge.
- *Belief*: knowledge occurs for psychological reasons within the individual.
- *Truth*: knowledge is a product of agreement and coherence.

Within the lifelong learning sector, knowledge is not static. The various subject areas have witnessed their value changing according to political and economic priorities. The traditional curriculum has become transformed as an employability agenda has influenced the development of the curriculum. It can be argued that the current interpretation of knowledge with its emphasis upon employability is a consequence of the influence of neoliberal values.

Simmons (2010: 369) argues that policy-making processes in societies such as the UK are based on a number of assumptions about the nature of people and the role of the state. It is accepted that there are innate differences between individuals with respect to intelligence, motivation, and moral character. This difference between individuals is highlighted so that competition and market forces become integral features of the social world (Lauder *et al.*, 2006: 25). This vision of society links to the writing of Friedman and Friedman (1980) and Hayek (1976). Olssen *et al.* (2004) argue that the philosophical background of this approach to policy making links to Hume, Ricardo and Smith. Central to these philosophies is a belief in competitive individualism and the maximisation of the market (Saunders, 2010: 42). Critics of neoliberalism (e.g. Torres, 1998, 2008; Apple, 2001; Giroux, 2005; Harvey, 2005) have commented on the economic essence of neoliberalism and its consequences for social policies. These critics argue that the emphasis that is given to economic outcomes in neoliberal societies results in particular consequences for social, political, cultural and educational institutions. This argument is exemplified by Archer and Leathwood (2003), who draw attention to the neoliberal definition of 'high quality', with its focus on how students are employed once they graduate. Mayo (2013) argues that the emergence of the word 'competences' is now a dominant discourse in the lifelong learning sector with its implication that there ought to be a clear purpose to education that can in turn be 'measured'. Archer and Leathwood (2003) propose that the association of 'education' with 'employment' is a consequence of complex political and socio-economic processes. Harris and Islar (2013) argue that these complex political and socio-economic processes are generated from historical and political discourses in order to produce a new understanding (or synthesis) of the social world. This argument is supported by Williams (2013), who believes that the neoliberal notion of students as 'consumers of education' arises from a complex socio-cultural history.

References and further reading

Apple, M. (2001) Comparing neo-liberal projects and inequality in education, *Comparative Education*, 37(4), 409–23.

Archer, L. and Leathwood, C. (2003) Identities and inequalities in higher education, in L. Archer, M. Hutchings and A. Ross (eds.) *Higher Education and Social Class: Issues of Exclusion and Inclusion*. London: Routledge Falmer.

Brennan, J., Edmunds, R., Houston, M., Jary, D., Lebeau, Y., Osbourne, M. and Richardson, J.T.E. (2010) *Improving What is Learned at University: An Exploration of the Social and Organisational Diversity of University Education*. London: Routledge.

Coffield, F. (2006) *Running ever faster down the wrong road*. Inaugural Lecture, University of London Institute of Education, London.

Freire, P. (1973) *Education for Critical Consciousness*. New York: Seabury Press.

Freire, P. (1985) *The Politics of Education: Culture, Power and Liberation*. South Hadley, MA: Bergin & Garvey.

Freire, P. (1994) *Pedagogy of Hope: Reliving the Pedagogy of the Oppressed*. New York: Continuum.

Friedman, M. and Friedman, R.D. (1980) *Free to Choose*. London: Penguin.

Giroux, H. (2000) *Impure Acts*. London: Taylor & Francis.

Giroux, H. (2005) *The Terror of Neo-liberalism: Cultural Politics and the Promise of Democracy*. Boulder, CO: Paradigm.

Harris, L. and Islar, M. (2013) Neoliberalism, nature and changing modalities of environmental governance in contemporary Turkey, in Y. Atasoy (ed.) *Global Economic Crisis and the Politics of Diversity*. London: Palgrave Macmillan.

Harvey, D. (2005) *A Brief History of Neo-liberalism*. Oxford: Oxford University Press.

Hayek, F. (1976) *Law, Legislation and Liberty*, Vol. 2. London: Routledge & Kegan Paul.

Kant, I. (1781/2007) *Critique of Pure Reason* (trans. M. Weigelt). London: Penguin Books.

Lauder, H., Brown, P., Dillabough, J. and Halsey, A.H. (2006) The prospects for education: individualisation, globalisation and social change, in H. Lauder, P. Brown, J. Dillabough and A.H. Halsey (eds.) *Education, Globalisation and Social Change*. Oxford: Oxford University Press.

Lucas, N. (2007) The in-service training of adult literacy, numeracy and English for Speakers of Other Languages teachers in England: the challenges of a 'standards-led model', *Journal of In-Service Education*, 33(1), 125–42.

Mayo, P. (2013) *Echoes from Freire for a Critically Engaged Pedagogy*. London: Bloomsbury.

Morley, C. and Dunstan, J. (2013) A response to neoliberal challenges to field education, *Social Work Education*, 32(2), 141–56.

Olssen, M., Codd, J.A. and O'Neill, M.A. (2004) *Education Policy: Globalisation, Citizenship and Democracy*. London: Sage.

Saunders, D.B. (2010) Neoliberal ideology and public education in the United States, *Journal for Critical Education Policy Studies*, 8(1), 42–77.

Simmons, R. (2010) Globalisation, neo-liberalism and vocational learning: the case of further education colleges, *Research in Post-Compulsory Education*, 15(4), 363–76.

Torres, C.A. (1998) *Democracy, Education and Multiculturalism*. Lanham, MD: Rowman & Littlefield.

Torres, C.A. (2008) *Education and Neoliberal Globalisation*. New York: Taylor & Francis.

Urban, M. (2008) Dealing with uncertainty: challenges and possibilities for the early childhood profession, *European Early Childhood Education Research Journal*, 16(2), 135–52.

Williams, J. (2013) *Consuming Higher Education: Why Learning Can't be Bought*. London: Bloomsbury.

L

Learners
Learning
Learning styles
Lesson planning
Liberal tradition
Lifelong learning

Learners

Learners are the students who form such an essential part of the lifelong learning sector. They are a diverse range of individuals. From older people who are learning in the community to 14-year-olds undertaking vocational programmes in colleges, our learners help to shape the particular nature of the lifelong learning sector. Learners are in need of learning (or changing their current views on the world). Whether they are 'able bodied' or have a disability, all learners are welcome to join the lifelong learning sector. It is often difficult to separate 'learners' from 'learning' as they go hand in hand in the central purpose of the lifelong learning sector.

There are several pedagogical strategies that exist to help our learners in their task of achieving 'deep learning':

- *Create intrinsic motivation.* Intrinsic motivation is interest in the subject and the tasks in themselves. Try to develop curiosity, interest, passion and 'real-world implications' in your teaching. Try to develop learning activities that are based on creativity, problem solving and individual responses to the pedagogical materials.
- *Learner activity.* Students need to be 'active' rather than 'passive' learners if they are to enjoy learning. Activities ought to be planned, reflected upon and processed.

- *Interaction with others.* Group work requires negotiating meaning, expressing and manipulating ideas. Discussion can be used to promote high-quality learning.
- *Establish a good knowledge base.* Without existing concepts, it would be impossible to make sense of new concepts. It is vital that the learner's existing knowledge and experience are brought out in the learning process. The structure of the topic must be made clear so that the learning process can be understood.

A number of practical strategies are available to encourage deep learning in our learners. It is important to ensure that the learners experience pedagogy that is based on 'teaching by asking' as opposed to 'teaching by telling'. Learners appear to benefit from what is referred to as the 'pose, pause, and pounce' technique. In other words, ask a question and wait for a response before then using that response to develop the learning process. The following pedagogical strategy can help to develop deep learning:

1. Think carefully about a clear question and write the question down.
2. Divide the learners into groups to work on answering the question.
3. Get feedback from the learners.
4. Write up the best ideas.
5. 'Top up' the learners' understanding of the key concepts that are being explored.
6. Summarise the main learning goals.

This pedagogical strategy is based on a 'problem-centred approach'. As opposed to teaching 'content', the learners ought to be given a challenge and then be expected to study this content in order to provide a solution to the problem. Deep learning involves the critical analysis of new ideas. These ideas ought to link to previously known concepts and principles. This in turn helps to develop understanding and long-term retention of concepts so that the learning process can be used for problem solving in unfamiliar contexts. Bloom (1956) outlines that deep learning promotes understanding and allows the learning process to be applied to a variety of contexts. In contrast, surface learning is the tacit acceptance that information is 'isolated' and not connected to a profound level of learning. The learning process becomes characterised by a superficial retention of material and there is no promotion of understanding or long-term retention of knowledge and information. Applying such techniques to our learners rests at the heart of teaching and learning in the lifelong learning sector.

Learning

There are many different definitions of learning, definitions that are informed by psychology, social psychology, anthropology and neuroscience. The use of additional prefixes – adult learning, informal learning, experiential learning, reflective learning – makes coming to an unambiguous definition yet more complicated. Dictionaries provide a general, if superficial start: 'knowledge acquired by study' is a typical dictionary definition. An analysis of the different definitions offered by educational researchers and writers would bring up many more, more or less different, definitions. Nonetheless, running through the many definitions that are present in the extant literature are a number of key themes, which in turn can be seen to influence pedagogic practice:

- *Learning is inferred from changes in behaviour.* Changes in behaviour might refer to how someone performs or discusses a particular task or how someone writes or talks about a particular body of knowledge. Assessment is the most conspicuous element of pedagogic practice through which these changes might be inferred.
- *Learning occurs as the result of given experiences that precede changes in behaviour.* Within the context of the lifelong learning sector, the kinds of experience that would precede changes in behaviour (and, therefore, learning) would include formal teaching sessions, coaching, work-based learning, tuition and so forth.
- *Learning involves behaviour potentiality* – that is, the capacity to perform some act at a future time, to be able to repeat something, as contrasted with performance that concerns the translation of potentiality into behaviour. Different theories of learning all share a concern to predict future capacity for performance. Ideas such as 'practice', 'repetition', and 'reinforcement' all revolve around the issue of how a change in behaviour can be understood as being more than a 'one-off'.
- *The modification of behaviour involved in learning is of a relatively permanent nature.* Common sense tells us that people forget things over time – in part due to the ageing process, but also due to forgetting as a result of not practising or reinforcing. The prevalence of 'refresher' courses, on the one hand, and of 'continuing professional development' courses, on the other, are examples of educational provision that assume that without regular reinforcement or practice, knowledge, competencies, and skills can be forgotten.

The different prefixes that are often applied serve to inform the reader as to the broader theoretical perspective that the writer or user of the term in question is discussing or subscribes to, assuming that the terms have been used correctly (educational practice is rife with terms that are misapplied and otherwise poorly employed, leading to 'conceptual slippage': 'communities of practice' is a stand-out example). For example, the term 'experiential learning' relates to the theories of David Kolb; 'situated learning' relates to the theories of Jean Lave and Etienne Wenger; 'expansive learning' relates to the theories of Yrgo Engeström. These three examples (and there are many others) are all – self-evidently – concerned with learning and ultimately have more in common than not. But there are some significant differences between these three approaches that require the practitioner who may choose to draw on them, to conceptualise her or his teaching practice in particular ways.

Here, we define learning as 'the apparent modification of a person's behaviour through his activities and experiences, so that his knowledge, skills and attitudes, including modes of adjustment, towards his environment are changed, more or less permanently' (Curzon and Tummons, 2013: 7). But it is important to stress that many definitions remain – in part, a reflection of the complexity of the subject matter and, in part, a reflection of the failure of the educational research community to build theory in a cumulative fashion and instead generate a multiplicity of theories, models, and concepts, the differences between some of which are more or less valid (Thomas, 2007).

Learning styles

At first glance, learning styles theories offer a 'personalised' way of under-standing student learning. According to learning styles theories (of which there are a considerable number – an issue that will be returned to shortly), any individual student in a workshop or classroom (or anywhere for that matter) will hold or exhibit particular preferences regarding how they learn. Put simply, some people prefer practical, 'hands-on' learning activities, whereas others prefer the theoretical; some people learning by seeing, while others prefer learning by listening, and so on. Students can ascertain their learning styles preferences, it is argued, through completing a learning styles question-naire or audit – a form of self-assessment that allows the student to identify how they like to learn best, according to the particular learning styles theory that the questionnaire rests upon. And in turn the motivation of students to engage in their learning can be raised if the ways in which their teachers prepare and deliver their sessions in such that they can be matched to the students' learning styles.

Learning styles theories thus purport to offer students and teachers a powerful way of exploring, and hence maximising, student learning. They have in recent years been widely used across the further and adult educa-tion sectors. Students are often asked to complete learning styles inventories as part of their programme of studies, and the results placed within their individual learning plans. Learning styles theories are also discussed in staff development sessions and sometimes in teacher training programmes. In some further education colleges, institutional *lesson plan* templates require the teacher or trainer to indicate how different learning styles have been accounted for during the lesson in question.

Although there are many different learning styles theories, a few are relatively prominent in the lifelong learning sector. Two particularly common models include the Honey and Mumford model, which categorises learners as activists, reflectors, theorists and pragmatists; and the Fleming model, which categorises learners as visual, auditory or kinaesthetic and is thus known as the VAK model.

However, the fundamental weaknesses of any learning styles approach are not difficult to ascertain, not least since there are so many different (more than 70) learning styles theories in circulation. Very few of these theories rest on any meaningful educational research and only a minority of them suggest that what the student should do is work to improve those 'kinds' of learning that, according to the responses to a learning styles questionnaire, make up an area of weakness. Indeed, one of the more powerful critiques of a learning styles approach in the classroom or workshop is that it runs the risk of labelling students (as 'pragmatists', or as 'auditory') in such a way that the kinds of pedagogic strategies that are employed are reduced, restricting opportunities to participate when – ironically – claiming to enhance learning.

Criticisms of learning styles do not only relate to their perceived negative impact on teaching practice, but also to the construction of the theories themselves. At the same time as many of the theories would appear to rest on minimal empirical research, it would appear that the vast majority of learning styles approaches are neither sufficiently valid nor reliable as forms of diagnostic assessment – that is, the questionnaires and other instruments used to assess an individual's learning styles do not provide reliable or repeatable results. And a final criticism is that learning styles theories fail to take account of *what* is being learned, thereby failing to acknowledge the impact on pedagogic practice of the content of the curriculum. Thus, for example, those learners who are (incorrectly) labelled as 'hands-on', are pushed towards those curricula that are similarly – and often equally incorrectly – labelled as being 'hands-on'. Even a brief evaluation of a motor vehicle or beauty therapy curriculum can show how both rest on bodies of professional knowledge as well as 'hands-on' aptitude.

Lesson planning

Writing a lesson plan is one of the most immediately recognisable bureaucratic tasks that teachers and trainers in the lifelong learning sector have to do. But it is important not to confuse the job of writing a lesson plan (which can be time consuming, even tedious) with lesson planning, which is a vital professional task. Planning a lesson would normally require consideration of:

- the specific aims of the session;
- how this session fits in to the broader aims of the course or module as a whole;
- the subjects or topics to be covered during the session;
- the resources or equipment that will be available;
- the nature of the student group;
- the different activities that will undertaken by the tutor and the students, which may include assessment activities;
- approximate timings for these activities.

In relation to the availability of resources and equipment, if some students are working in pairs and taking turns with specialist equipment, other activities will need to be prepared to keep the others busy while they wait their turn. Very few further education colleges have enough CNC milling machines in their engineering workshops to allow a group of 12 students to all be working on one at the same time, for example. In a session where ICT is being used, it is sensible to make sure that all of the machines are switched on and, if possible, logged on before the session starts. Waiting for PCs to warm up can be frustrating and, if one machine crashes, the session might be disrupted. If students are going to make some posters, perhaps as a formative assessment exercise, the teacher must make sure that there are enough pens, paper, and Blu-Tack. Dealing with issues such as these requires common sense, and a good awareness of the facilities that are available to you within the institution where you work.

Some planning issues require a different kind of professional knowledge. To plan appropriately for the session aims, the content and how it will fit into the course or module as a whole, it is important to be familiar with the curricular documents that have been supplied by the awarding body responsible for the course. Planning processes will require a good degree of familiarity with the requirements of the curriculum in terms of specified content, assessment criteria, key transferable skills and such like. Other planning issues rest on more theoretical knowledge. A consideration of the nature of the student group, and how this will impact on the planning of the session, might lead to a discussion of the ways in which the profile of the students, in terms of age, ethnicity, prior experience or ability, might impact on group dynamics. It might lead to a consideration of issues that affect student motivation, or behaviour (a particularly relevant issue for tutors who work with students aged 14–16). The needs of students with seen or unseen disabilities will have to be accounted for. All of these issues might have an impact on the decisions that we make about which resources to use, how those resources might be designed, or which activities to try.

No matter how exhaustive the planning process, it is important to remember that the plan itself is not set in stone. By treating plans as a series of cues or prompts, rather than a series of rigid instructions, teachers can be confident that time and effort have gone into thinking about what the students will do that day, while at the same time being aware of the need to be flexible during the session itself. It is hard to predict how our students will respond to an activity. A responsive practitioner will be aware of how well – or not – a session is proceeding, and will be able to adapt accordingly. This might involve changing the running order of items, or allowing a discussion to continue beyond its planned time, or turning a tutor-led activity into one led by a student group.

Liberal tradition

The liberal tradition in adult education is a philosophy of education that stands in stark opposition to the target-driven new vocationalism that characterises current provision within the lifelong learning sector. Rather than focusing on employability, the liberal tradition focuses on education as a necessary component of being an active and reflective citizen. Instead of organising access to different areas of the curriculum through examination-based selection criteria, the liberal tradition instead demands that any programme of study is open to anyone who wishes to attend. The roots of the liberal tradition can be most easily seen in the work of Albert Mansbridge, founder of the Workers' Educational Association, who argued for wider access to the 'elite' curricula of the universities for working people, and in the work of other important adult educators of the twentieth century, including E.P. Thompson (the author of *The Making of the English Working Class*). Ultimately, it finds its roots in liberalism, here understood as a philosophy of individual freedom and self-motivation aligned to knowledgeable involvement in social, political and civic life. Within an educational context, the liberal tradition rests on two key elements. First, there is a commitment to education that promotes an inquiring and questioning response and attitudes and, by extension, encourages people to be inquiring and questioning in other areas of their lives. Second, there is a commitment to a pedagogy that rests on dialogue and on the 'Socratic' model of debate and discussion.

The key tenets of the liberal tradition in adult education can be understood as follows (Taylor, 1996):

1.   The curriculum ought to be based on the liberal arts – subjects such as literature, philosophy, and history – not on subjects that are

written into curricula solely to direct students to become better, more effective workers.

2. Learning is not 'learning for learning's sake' (in contrast to Mansbridge). Instead, learning should be understood as being focused on the intrinsically important issues of life and of human society.

3. Because the liberal tradition is non-vocational, it rejects formal assessment, examination, and certification. The liberal tradition does not seek to enrol the process of education within any form of target setting or culture of evaluation or measurement.

4. The liberal tradition is democratic – therefore, it does not seek to exclude anyone who wishes to become involved. There are no formal selection procedures.

5. The liberal tradition values a dialogic pedagogy: the small seminar group is argued to be the most effective educational strategy.

The contemporary focus on employability, vocationalism, transferable skills, and such like notwithstanding, the liberal tradition can be seen as anachronistic in a number of ways. Criticisms have centred on the naïve optimism of the liberal tradition, of the limited nature of the liberal curriculum, of the Victorian paternalism that characterised the attitudes of tutors and of the individualistic and uncommitted nature of the student body, in sharp contrast to the idealistic, socially and politically engaged student body envisioned by advocates of the liberal tradition (Mayo and Thompson, 1995). At the same time, however, although the liberal tradition is gone and almost forgotten in the lifelong learning sector, the broad notion that opportunities for adult education should be as widely available as possible and free of the paraphernalia of formal accreditation and assessment speaks to the notion that learning should be about 'more than' qualifications, that there are *wider benefits* to learning that should not be ignored.

Lifelong learning

The concept of 'lifelong learning' is a generous term that refers to a number of different issues, practices or ideas. It can be used to refer to informal or recreational learning provision (such as those provided by the Workers' Educational Association). It can be used to refer to the (usually part-time) *outreach* programmes offered by universities. And it can be used to refer to the provision of *work-based* learning or *professional learning* for people seeking to move into or within employment. Ideas about lifelong learning have changed over recent years and decades in response to two main drivers. First, there are changing ideas about what education and training should be 'for'; for example, should it always be linked to employment? But there are also changing political and economic discourses in relation to education and training; for example, can education and training be used to help influence other areas of social policy?

A brief consideration of changing employment patterns allows this issue to be unpacked. As changes in employment or career structure are increasingly common for an increasing number of workers, so the need for people either in or seeking employment to gain new skills or update existing skills has become more pressing. At the same time, employers seek to develop workforces that are increasingly 'flexible' – able to perform more than one role or fill more than one position within the organisation. In these different contexts, the need to 'retrain' or to 'reskill' or 'upskill' is common. In this sense, lifelong learning is concerned solely with sustaining the employability of the individual, who is positioned as being responsible for their own (re)training and, by extension, their own current or future employment. More people have to remain – or once again become – learners for longer periods of time in adult life. A different, though related notion of lifelong learning is wrapped up inside social policy initiatives, particularly those relating to social exclusion that were a characteristic feature of the policies of the UK Labour government from 1997 to 2010. Policy discourses such as these linked economic growth and aspiration with perceived social problems, suggesting that if more people took part in lifelong learning – as a way of ensuring future employment – then the economic benefits that would accrue would lead in turn to wider social benefits, and would contribute to the growth of 'social justice' (itself a contested concept).

Arguments such as these that attach lifelong learning to economic prosperity and job stability are far removed from the liberal tradition that characterised adult and continuing education during the late nineteenth and early to mid-twentieth centuries, which foregrounded learning 'for its own sake', as a cultural and social benefit in its own right. Provision such as this has declined quite markedly over the last 20 years or so, although the Workers' Educational Association still offers such courses. Some higher education provision is also tailored to lifelong learning, through the provision of part-time provision, often leading to direct access to full-time degree schemes, franchised awards delivered in conjunction with further education colleges (usually referred to as higher education in further education or HE in FE). The continuing professional development requirements that many professions subscribe to are another example of lifelong learning, again directly linked to employability; in this context, the need to remain up to date in one's field of competence. Very few people have a 'job for life'. In order to participate fully in society, other forms of further learning may also be needed – the proliferation of computer courses, linked to notions of a 'digital divide', is an obvious example. Perhaps it is indeed right to say that in some ways, many – if not all – of us are 'lifelong learners'.

References and further reading

Bloom, B.S. (1956) *Taxonomy of Educational Objectives: The Classification of Educational Goals – Handbook I: Cognitive Domain*. New York: McKay.

Coffield, F., Moseley, D., Hall, E. and Ecclestone, K. (2004) *Should We be Using Learning Styles? What Research has to Say to Practice*. London: Learning and Skills Research Centre.

Curry, L. (1990) A critique of the research on learning styles, *Educational Leadership*, 48(2), 50–6.

Curzon, L. and Tummons, J. (2013) *Teaching in Further Education: An Outline of Principles and Practice* (7th edn.). London: Bloomsbury.

Hargreaves, D. (2005) *About Learning*. London: Demos.

Mayo, M. and Thompson, J. (eds.) (1995) *Adult Learning, Critical Intelligence and Social Change*. Leicester: NIACE.

Taylor, R. (1996) Preserving the liberal tradition in new times, in J. Wallis (ed.) *Liberal Adult Education: The End of an Era?* Nottingham: University of Nottingham.

Thomas, G. (2007) *Education and Theory: Strangers in Paradigms*. Maidenhead: McGraw-Hill/Open University Press.

Thompson, E.P. (1963) *The Making of the English Working Class*. New York: Vintage Books.

Tummons, J. (2010) The assessment of lesson plans in teacher education: a case study in assessment validity and reliability, *Assessment and Evaluation in Higher Education*, 35(7), 847–57.

M

Mentees
Mentors
Mixed Economy Group, and HE in FE
Motivation

Mentees

The reality of the lifelong learning sector experience appears to be that whether full time or part time, the teaching staff can experience a challenging few months of teaching and meeting programme targets. The intensity of the process can mean that lifelong learning sector staff are often unable to reflect fully on their developmental journey to qualified professional status. Brookes (2005: 45) cites Foster (2001) to argue that this is a result of the lack of a 'systematic monitoring of the training process'. This argument has been used to develop the mentor–mentee role in lifelong learning.

According to Ingleby and Hunt (2008: 63) and Hobson (2002: 5), there are three main factors that have led to mentoring in the lifelong learning sector becoming such an important area of debate. These factors are legislative (or standards driven), pedagogical and a product of student experience. Hobson (2002: 5) draws attention to legislation such as Department for Education Circular 9/92 (DfE, 1992), which has seen mentoring become an important component of teacher training. The consequence of this circular has been that student teachers on postgraduate courses spend two-thirds of their course within teaching contexts. In a training environment in which initial teacher training (ITT) in England is expected to follow the lead of school-based teacher training – a point revealed through the curriculum changes for PCET teacher training proposed in 2007 by Lifelong Learning UK (LLUK) and Standards Verification UK (SVUK) – this legislative (or standards-driven) development has increased the importance of mentors working alongside trainee teachers. It would appear, however, that the standards-driven aspect of the development is having a negative impact on the nature of the mentoring experience.

Hobson (2002: 6) and Ingleby and Hunt (2008: 63) note that changes in pedagogy have also raised the importance of the mentor–mentee relationship. As opposed to appearing to be 'a sage on the stage', the pedagogical focus appears increasingly to be on being 'a guide on the side'. This mirrors the Ofsted change of focus from 'teaching' to 'learning'. It means that there is increasing interest in how skills are developed through 'coaching' as opposed to 'teaching' (Sloboda, 1986: 32–3) alongside the continuing influence of Vygotskian and Rogerian paradigms of learning (Hobson, 2002: 6). The consequence has been an increased interest in the humanistic processes that enable the development of professional skills. It can be argued that instead of listening to a 'master', the focus is now on the pedagogical processes that characterise the interaction between 'master' and 'apprentice'.

Hobson (2002: 6) goes on to highlight 'the conceptions of those who are seeking to become teachers' as another factor that has contributed to the recent heightened interest in mentoring. These students have been identified as having clear expectations that they would be allocated a mentor to help them in their training. Hobson found that 92.4 per cent of 277 ITT students thought that it would be 'very valuable' or 'essential' to plan lessons with a mentor. Moreover, these students noted the importance of combining this mentor support with feedback from university tutors (Hobson, 2002: 6).

This appears to suggest that although the concept of mentoring is not a recent one, its importance as an aspect of the lifelong learning sector has increased in recent years. It is deemed as being a desirable component of ITT both by student teachers and Ofsted. This point is reinforced by Chambers *et al.* (2001), who argue that 'a lack of support' is an important reason why student teachers fail to complete their ITT courses.

Mentors

Mentoring has been a key aspect of the lifelong learning sector for a number of years. In 2002, the Department for Education and Skills (DfES) introduced 'Success for All' as a way of reforming the English lifelong learning sector. This reform resulted in the development of PCET ITT mentoring. Moreover, a Standards Unit was established to disseminate best practice. The survey of teacher training that was undertaken by Ofsted in 2002–2003 identified that taught modules on teacher training programmes were not necessarily linked to practical teaching and that mentoring was not as well developed as it could be for PCET ITT programmes. This led the DfES Standards Unit to introduce a consultation document in 2003 that recommended having mentors for trainees and new teachers working in PCET. The implications from both Ofsted and the Standards Unit appeared to be that all would be well in PCET ITT if a system of mentoring were established similar to that for school teacher training. Hankey (2004: 390) argues that the irony of this implication is that informal mentoring has occurred within the PCET for years. Moreover, Hankey (2004: 390) goes on to make the critical point that the simplistic assumption that all can be well in PCET ITT if the school mentoring system is followed is not likely to work due to the 'unique complexity' of PCET.

Hankey (2004: 391) claims that the development of PCET ITT mentoring has been based on a hybrid of two of Maynard and Furlong's (1993) models for mentoring. The ideal mentor is assumed to be both an 'expert' and a 'critical friend'. The key debate that has subsequently emerged within the current PCET ITT mentoring system is the extent to which the mentoring relationship ought to be supportive of the professional development of the trainees as opposed to judging the quality of their teaching. Moreover, the emergence of a model of mentoring that is similar to Daloz's (1986) 'support' and 'challenge' approach appears to lend itself to judging teaching ability and not necessarily developing reflective practice. This variability of interpretation of the purpose of mentoring is at the heart of previous research on PCET ITT mentoring (Hankey, 2004; Ingleby and Hunt, 2008; Tedder and Lawy, 2009; Ingleby, 2010, 2011).

Ingleby and Tummons (2012) argue that mentoring is a helpful part of the lifelong learning sector. It is argued that new staff in particular can benefit from the mentoring process. It is helpful to have colleagues who can offer help and advice about teaching and learning strategies. The challenge appears to be finding a model of mentoring that is developmental in nature. In Ingleby and Tummons' (2012) research, this style of mentoring model is advocated. In contrast, the Ofsted model appears to be based on 'judging' the teaching ability of the mentees. Research on mentoring appears to show that neither mentors nor mentees welcome this judgemental model of mentoring. In contrast to associating mentoring with inspection, Ingleby (2010, 2011), Ingleby and Hunt (2008) and Tedder and Lawy (2009) propose that PCET ITT mentoring should encourage the development of reflective practice. If these arguments are combined with the recommendations of Minott (2010), a vision emerges of a mentoring system that is based on the ultimate goal of facilitating self-directed professional development. Surely this would be a way of developing professional practice within this particular educational context?

Mixed Economy Group, and HE in FE

The Mixed Economy Group (MEG) is an organisation that represents 41 further education colleges that also offer higher education provision (usually referred to as higher education in further education – HE in FE).

Almost four-fifths of further education colleges in England and Wales offer HE in FE provision (but many of these offer only a very small number of courses), predominantly on a part-time basis, and HE in FE students constitute almost 10 per cent of the entire higher education student population. Although HE in FE students represent a minority of the student body within colleges in numerical terms, the HE in FE curriculum is important in terms of both the *widening participation* routes that it offers, and the *professional learning* opportunities that college-based higher education provides. As such, HE in FE provision more generally makes a broad and significant contribution to the wider lifelong learning agenda.

HE in FE provision is divided into two main areas: prescribed higher education and non-prescribed higher education. Prescribed higher education refers to all of the provision within colleges that is awarded by higher education institutions (HEIs) – universities and university colleges. Such provision typically includes foundation degrees (which were first introduced in 2001, and which upon completion can allow students access to 'mainstream' higher education to 'top up' to a full honours degree), certificates or diplomas of higher education, and Higher National Certificates and Diplomas (HNCs and HNDs). The Higher Education Funding Council for England (HEFCE) funds these programmes either indirectly via a working arrangement with a nearby university or directly to the college. Non-prescribed higher education includes programmes at Level 4 or above offered by awarding bodies such as City & Guilds (which offer a range of higher level NVQs), as well as professional programmes relating to areas such as the law (e.g. the Professional Higher Diploma in Law and Practice offered by the Chartered Institute of Legal Executives) and accountancy (e.g. the Diploma in Accountancy offered by the Association of Accounting Technicians). The MEG provides a platform for policy and practice discussions relating to these distinct and diverse forms of higher education provision, covering issues relevant to local employers, widening access, funding and curriculum design. HE in FE provision is diverse, therefore, in terms of organisational or institutional context, student profile and curriculum. It is the contribution that HE in FE makes to widening participation that provides a common thread. College-based HE in FE provision is overwhelmingly part time, invariably based on admissions policies that allow access to applicants with non-standard entry qualifications, and predominantly offering vocational and professional curricula that are aligned to the world of work. This overwhelming focus on vocational and professional curricula makes HE in FE provision quite distinct from that offered by both older and newer universities.

The nature and demands of HE in FE provision have implications for the staff involved in teaching on these programmes and for the quality assurance (QA) measures that colleges have to abide by. Some colleges have teaching and management staff who work across both further and higher education curricula. Other colleges, particularly those with a larger portfolio of higher education courses, have staff who engage in scholarly activity and who teach solely or predominantly on higher education courses, dedicated resources for higher education students, and dedicated managers who focus on the QA requirements of the Higher Education Review (HER) rather than on those of Ofsted. These colleges are, it is suggested, more able to demonstrate the development of an 'ethos of higher education', which is distinct from that of further education, but which is, at the same time, not simply a copy of what happens in universities themselves.

Motivation

Motivation has been defined by psychologists as involving a person's drive and goal-seeking behaviour, and the internal state that results in behaviour directed towards a specific goal. In the context of this book, it refers to a person's willingness or desire to participate in education or training. Maslow's hierarchy of needs is a popular theory of motivation in the lifelong learning sector. But it is a theory that attempts to categorise motivation as a discrete quality or characteristic of the individual person, rather than focusing on what factors – environmental, social, political – motivate or demotivate people. Moreover, much of Maslow's theorising appears to be based on insubstantial speculation. Rather than conducting thorough and robust research, he drew on colourful anecdotes, selective case reporting and inconclusive observations (Illeris, 2007).

Other educational psychologists have proposed a number of types of motivation that relate to student attitudes to participating in education and training, and that can be seen to come from both within and outside the individual. Different categories of motivation are reported in the literature:

1. *Instrumental motivation.* This type of motivation, which is a response to an external pressure, can be seen when students participate solely because of the likely consequences. For example, completing a course might lead to a tangible reward (such as a new job) or avoiding a negative consequence (such as redundancy).
2. *Social motivation.* Students influenced by this type of motivation tend to participate so as to please those they respect or admire. The reward here is not a material one, and is instead related to the relationship between the student and the person whose praise or approval is considered important.
3. *Intrinsic motivation.* In this context, there are no external rewards. Instead, students participate for the pleasure and satisfaction that the

learning brings. Intrinsic motivation appears to be a crucial element of high-quality involvement in education and training. Curiosity and a willingness to take on challenges may characterise the attitude and approach to learning of students motivated in this way.

The understanding and management of student motivation within further education raises a number of issues that are distinct from those faced by teachers in the compulsory sectors. In part, this is due to the persistence of stereotypical assumptions regarding the reasons why students choose to attend further education programmes. Put simply, there continues to be an assumption that because students have 'chosen' to attend further education college, and because they have left behind the formal schooling that they were 'unsuited' for, they will be motivated to study in further education. Stereotypes are also found in relation to adult learners, whose motivation towards study – simply because 'they are adults' – is also taken for granted. In fact, in both contexts such assumptions should be avoided, and it is only through a more meaningful dialogue, and a process of 'coming to know' the students, that reasons for engaging in learning and hence attitudes and levels of motivation towards learning can be established.

It is important for the teacher or trainer to recognise signs of declining motivation at an early stage. Low motivation can act to promote behaviour that might be more or less disruptive, or even overtly hostile, which may cause wider problems in the workshop or seminar room. There are a number of behaviours that can indicate a decline in motivation, including: poor class attendance; a consistent lack of punctuality; arriving at a lesson without appropriate books or equipment; refusal or reluctance to take part in question-and-answer sessions; reluctance to take part in a practical demonstration; missing deadlines for assignments; talking loudly and out of turn; using a mobile phone.

References and further reading

Brookes, W. (2005) The graduate teacher programme in England: mentor training, quality assurance and the findings of inspection, *Journal of In-Service Education*, 31(1), 43–61.

Chambers, G., Coles, J. and Roper, T. (2001) *Students withdrawing from PGCE (secondary) courses*. Paper presented at the British Educational Research Association Annual Conference, University of Leeds, Leeds, 13–15 September.

Curzon, L. and Tummons, J. (2013) *Teaching in Further Education: An Outline of Principles and Practice* (7th edn.). London: Bloomsbury.

Daloz, J. (1986) *Effective Mentoring and Teaching*. San Francisco, CA: Jossey-Bass.

Department for Education (DfE) (1992) *The New Requirements for Initial Teacher Training* (Circular 9/92). London: DfE.

Department for Education and Skills (DfES) (2002) *Success for All*. London: DfES.

Duckworth, V., Flanagan, K., McCormack, K. and Tummons, J. (2012) *Understanding Behaviour, 14+*. Maidenhead: McGraw-Hill.

Foster, R. (2001) *The graduate teacher route to QTS – motorway, by-way or by-pass?* Paper presented at the British Educational Research Association Annual Conference, University of Leeds, Leeds, 13–15 September.

Hankey, J. (2004) The good, the bad and other considerations: reflections on mentoring trainee teachers in post-compulsory education, *Research in Post-Compulsory Education*, 9(3), 389–400.

Hobson, A.J. (2002) Student teachers' perceptions of school-based mentoring in initial teacher training (ITT), *Mentoring and Tutoring*, 10(1), 5–20.

Illeris, K. (2007) *How We Learn*. London: Routledge.

Ingleby, E. (2010) Robbing Peter to pay Paul: the price of standards-driven education, *Research in Post-Compulsory Education*, 15(1), 427–41.

Ingleby, E. (2011) Asclepius or Hippocrates? Differing interpretations of post-compulsory initial teacher training mentoring, *Journal of Vocational Education and Training*, 63(1), 15–25.

Ingleby, E. and Hunt, J. (2008) The CPD needs of mentors in post-compulsory initial teacher training in England, *Journal of In-Service Education*, 34(1), 61–74.

Ingleby, E. and Tummons, J. (2012) Repositioning professionalism: teachers, mentors, policy and praxis, *Research in Post-Compulsory Education*, 17(2), 163–79.

Maynard, T. and Furlong, J. (1993) Learning to teach and models of mentoring, in D. McIntyre, H. Hagger and M. Wilkin (eds.) *Mentoring: Perspectives on School-based Teacher Education*. London: Kogan Page.

Minott, M.A. (2010) Reflective teaching as self-directed professional development: building practical or work-related knowledge, *Professional Development in Education*, 36(2), 325–38.

Sloboda, J. (1986) Acquiring skill, in A. Gellatley (ed.) *The Skilful Mind: An Introduction to Cognitive Psychology*. Milton Keynes: Open University Press.

Tedder, M. and Lawy, R. (2009) The pursuit of 'excellence': mentoring in further education initial teacher training in England, *Journal of Vocational Education and Training*, 61(4), 413–29.

N

NEETS

NEETS

A 'NEET' is a person who is 'not in employment, education or training'. The acronym originates in the UK but it is also used in other countries. In the UK, the acronym refers to individuals who are aged 16–24. Those aged 16–18 tend to be of particular concern to politicians and policy makers. The onus for addressing the problem posed by NEETs appears to be on the lifelong learning sector.

Since the lifelong learning sector is associated with the provision of vocational opportunities and skills development, the sector has become associated with the provision of skills to help young people not in employment, education or training contribute to the economy. In 2007, a report commissioned by the Prince's Trust identified that a fifth of 16- to 24-year-olds in England, Scotland and Wales were not in employment, education or training. In 2011, such youngsters accounted for 16.2 per cent of this age group. The number of individuals who are in this category appears to be one reason why this acronym is increasingly recognised. It can be argued that it is not right to refer to young people in this way. The term 'NEET' may be used in a derogatory way. Instead of recognising that these young people are in need of opportunities, they may be perceived as being part of the problem. Rogers (2004) would argue that in this instance the use of the term NEET is likely to increase the 'would/should dilemma' (and the subsequent anxiety) of these young people.

That there are young people not in employment, education or training in the UK reveals a contradiction in British society: alongside those labelled 'NEET' are youngsters not so labelled. Karl Marx popularised the notion of looking at the contradictory elements of social systems. Marx also popularised the terms 'infrastructure' and 'superstructure'. Whereas the infrastructure refers to all tangible aspects of the economic system, the superstructure refers to systems of belief and ideas. According to Marx, this economic infrastructure is responsible for shaping the beliefs and ideas of the superstructure. Marx also popularised the idea of social classes. The traditional Marxist emphasis is on the existence of two main social groups, a ruling class and a subject class that are considered to be in conflict with each other. Marx argued that there are fundamental contradictions within modern industrial societies such as the UK. The exemplification of such contradictory relationships can be seen in the traditional working arrangements for factories. Whereas the workers are traditionally 'on the factory floor', the factory manager is usually based in a private office. Another example of a contradictory relationship occurs with private ownership. A few powerful individuals own companies whereas the majority of the population own very little compared with these powerful individuals. Marx argues that the many contradictions in society produce instability and conflict. This is the rationale behind the prediction that a revolution will occur within capitalist societies so that the social order can be refined into a communist way of life.

Audi (1999) argues that Marxism is a profound and complex social theory. The emphasis on 'conflict' is testimony to the influence of Hegel's philosophical idea of the social world being characterised by 'thesis, antithesis, and synthesis'. It is acknowledged that a social revolution will only occur when the working class become fully aware of the unfair contradictions that exist within the social system. The argument runs that until there is this realisation, the social system is likely to survive because of the 'false consciousness' of the working class. It is only when the working class becomes fully aware of the implications of social contradictions and of the need to replace the existing social order with a communist society that a social revolution will occur and the contradictory elements of society (like NEETS) will be resolved.

References and further reading

Audi, R. (1999) *The Cambridge Dictionary of Philosophy*. Cambridge: Cambridge University Press.

Rogers, C. (2004) *On Becoming a Person*. London: Constable.

O

Observations
Offender learning
Ofsted
Outreach

Observations

Observations are associated with formal assessments of teaching practice. These observations of teaching are a part of the process of quality assurance within the lifelong learning sector. The observations are often associated with Ofsted (Office for Standards in Education, Children's Services and Skills) during inspections of teaching across the lifelong learning sector but they are not confined to the inspection process. Before a formal inspection, there are often internal inspections of teaching within the lifelong learning setting. These graded observations have become part of the internal quality assurance processes of the lifelong learning settings. The grades that are given to teaching will include variations of 'outstanding', 'good', 'satisfactory' and 'unsatisfactory'.

The grading system that is used to observe teaching by Ofsted is controversial. The controversy concerns whether the process should be judgemental or developmental in its focus. Hankey (2004: 391) notes that the model that Ofsted favours is based on judging the quality of the teaching that is being observed. Moreover, the emergence of this model of observation is similar to Daloz's (1986) 'support' and 'challenge' approach. It appears to lend itself to judging teaching ability and not necessarily developing reflective practice.

However, Tedder and Lawy (2009) note that since 2003, Ofsted has viewed the observation process in a highly judgemental way (as opposed to viewing observations as being developmental). The Inspectorate appears to want to assess the impact of teaching on educational performance by measuring this performance against academic results. The variety of interpretations of the purpose of observations, however, reveals a difficulty with the Ofsted agenda

(Tedder and Lawy, 2009). It seems highly unlikely that all stakeholders will unilaterally accept the 'support' and 'challenge' model of observations when other (more appealing) models of observation are exist.

Lawy and Tedder (2011: 393) claim that, through Ofsted, successive governments have imposed the performative model of observation on the lifelong learning sector. The assumption appears to be based on the idea that 'bad' teaching can be improved through assessing the performance of teachers via observations in order to ensure 'world-class standards'. This has led to what Colley (2003) refers to as a 'triadic' relationship, since now a third party, Ofsted, has joined the 'dyadic' relationship between teacher and learner. Moreover, Lawy and Tedder (2011: 393) outline that there is no 'best practice' model for observing teaching. The critique of the 'support' and 'judge' model of mentoring rests in its inability to facilitate personal, social, and general pedagogical development.

Offender learning

Offender learning is part of the educational provision of the lifelong learning sector. It takes place in prisons with the realisation that many offenders have had little formal education. The attempts made at providing skills for the offenders have as their goal the hope that those offenders will not offend again in the future.

The following key ideas are of particular importance in offender learning:

- The basic skills of the offenders are regarded as being an educational priority.
- The acquisition of skills is equated with providing an opportunity to have a 'new life' beyond prison.
- A particular sort of teaching approach is used in offender learning. Unlike the police or prison guards, the educators are often viewed favourably by offenders. This positive appraisal of the teaching staff may enable the development of a humanist style of teaching and learning.
- Learners are provided with opportunities for philosophical thought and discussion where appropriate.
- Learners are involved in learning activities that challenge their existing knowledge and understanding in an appropriate way.

Offender learning is also associated with controversy. The acceptance of offender learning can depend upon the attitudes that individuals outside the prisons have towards offenders. Some in society have little time for offender learning, since they believe that prison is there to punish 'criminals', and the idea of offender learning is at odds with this view.

The ultimate goal of offender learning is to enable the offenders to reflect on their previous choices so that they make new decisions that will benefit themselves and society alike. In providing offenders with basic skills such as literacy and numeracy and ICT skills, it is hoped that they will be able to make a positive contribution to society rather than return to a life of crime. The merits of offender learning include:

- the pedagogical process provides the offenders with an opportunity to acquire skills they have not had before;
- learning may occur so that the offenders become changed individuals;
- teaching sessions enable the offenders to acquire employability.

The critics of offender education claim that the result is 'better educated criminals' who will still be involved with crime but in a more sophisticated way. It is, however, generally accepted that rates of recidivism (or re-offending) are reduced following prison education. A number of teachers are 'called' to prison education. This form of education is often regarded as being a 'vocation'. It is a demanding form of education in the lifelong learning sector, but it can be very rewarding making a difference to the lives of offenders. Those working in prison education require the 'softer skills' of being a 'guide on the side' (Petty, 2009), skills elaborated by Rogers (2004). The need to be 'empathetic' and 'congruent' with the offenders is a vital component of educating this group of learners effectively. The rewards stem from the realisation that there could not be a more needy group of learners. Prisons, however, can be harsh environments. It takes a particular sort of person to work in institutions that remove individuals' liberties.

Ofsted

The Office for Standards in Education (Ofsted) is the non-ministerial department of Her Majesty's Chief Inspector of Schools in England. Although the Inspectorate has existed since the mid-nineteenth century, it was reorganised significantly in 1992 under the Education (Schools) Act. Ofsted is also named explicitly in the Education and Inspections Act (2006). Ofsted inspectors are responsible for inspecting education in early years and beyond. A number of objections have been raised to the process of inspection. These objections include the concern that if an organisation is given notice of a forthcoming inspection, much of the organisation's focus goes into working out how to please the Inspectorate. The amount of notice given for an inspection has changed over the years. The current system offers little such notice, the idea being that the Inspectorate is able to see the establishment 'as it is'. Less preparation time is regarded as being a way of revealing the true nature of the establishment.

The role that Ofsted has in ensuring standards of high-quality teaching and learning is controversial. Is a one-week visit really going to help improve standards of teaching and learning? There is also concern over the methodology that is applied by Ofsted. Much of the decision making appears to be based upon statistical data regarding how effective the results of the establishment are. The variability in factors that contribute to this grading system, however, means that the allocation of grades is complicated. For example, Ofsted is interested in the achievement that is 'attained' based on the entry point of the learners and their abilities when they arrive. This appears to favour the admission of students with low ability, in order to show that their attainment has been significant! There are also concerns about the language used within the Ofsted inspection process. A grade of 'satisfactory' has become to be interpreted as meaning 'unsatisfactory'. Satisfactory has become quasi Orwellian-speak for not satisfactory at all!

The 'tension' and 'conflict' that is associated with Ofsted links to the ideas of Jürgen Habermas (1989). The tension that exists within many of the Ofsted inspection processes appears to justify the Habermasian understanding of the nature of 'advanced capitalist societies'. Habermas argues that modern capitalist societies such as the UK are subject to crises within the realm of ideas rather than within the economy. This is because the state is not perceived to be representative of all sectors of society even though there may be relative economic stability. For example, the education system is made up of a number of distinct and at times competing groups of learners that include 'early years', the '14–19 sector', and the 'higher education sector'. The tension that appears to exist between the teaching profession and the Ofsted Inspectorate is a further example of this 'tension in the realm of ideas'. There have been calls for Ofsted to be abolished. Based on the work of Urban (2008), we can see that Ofsted is a classic example of policy and practice being at odds with one another. As opposed to being an organisation 'for teachers', Ofsted is viewed as a means of 'punishing teachers'. Part of this critique is based on the perceived lack of encouragement of reflective practice. There are also calls for an inspection process that mirrors examples of good teaching and learning activities, as opposed to being based on what is happening in the classroom.

Outreach

Outreach is a broad term that is used to refer to a variety of practices, initiatives, and policies, all of which are designed in some way to encourage participation in education and training. Terms such as 'widening access' and 'widening participation' are commonly used within this context, and are used to describe a variety of responses to the needs of different groups who are under-represented in – or otherwise missing from – education and training:

- The provision of supporting structures such as subsidised childcare facilities or transport to and from a further education college.
- The use of off-site venues such as church halls or community centres to deliver programmes of learning 'in the community'.
- Cooperation with other service groups such as organisations working with ex-offenders or immigrants.
- The use of accreditation of prior leaning (APL) in order to allow students without traditional entry qualifications to access further and higher education programmes.
- The establishment of links between schools and local universities to encourage more young people to apply to university, through arranging visits to university campuses or visits to schools by students.

The rationales or philosophies that underpin initiatives established by successive governments to encourage a wider uptake of education have varied over time, but can be summarised in terms of the following key assumptions:

- a workforce with higher overall levels of qualifications will be more economically productive;
- access to education can alleviate issues of social inequality.

At the same time, however, it can be argued that the desire of successive governments to encourage more people to stay in education and training for longer rests on:

- the need to prevent too many younger people from entering the workforce too soon;
- the use of education and training provision as a relatively affordable proxy for more deep-seated social and economic issues.

In the light of issues such as these, it is arguably the case that much outreach and widening participation work rests on rather contradictory foundations. There is no doubting the sincerity and enthusiasm for practitioners who work with adult learners or other so-called 'hard-to-reach' groups (adult education practitioners, in particular, are invariably motivated by a commitment to 'social justice'), but it can be argued that the claims made for the efficacy of widening participation and outreach programmes are overstated. At an empirical level, the Wolf Report (2011) suggested that the majority of NVQ qualifications awarded at Levels 1 and 2 (which, typically, are those being taken by students who are most at risk from leaving education) failed either to lead to employment or to provide meaningful progression routes to higher level qualifications. At a policy level, it is difficult to reconcile the rhetoric of recent governments concerning the need to encourage students to stay in or return to education and training when the numbers of part-time higher education students have been in steady decline for the last decade and when the education maintenance allowance (EMA) for students in further education has been cut. And it is important to remember that the meaning of terms such as 'outreach' and 'widening participation' change over time. The changing nature of higher education provision in the UK provides a convenient example. The expansion of university provision of the 1960s (when the so-called 'plate glass' universities were established – Sussex, Lancaster, York, and Warwick, for example) was designed to encourage local economic growth in the areas chosen for the new universities as well as facilitate an expansion of university provision. These universities made up the 'widening participation' agenda of the time, and yet are now all classified as 'research-intensive', and in turn they now offer different kinds of outreach provision to 'non-traditional' students, while at the same time maintaining their positions as highly selective universities.

References and further reading

Colley, H. (2003) *Mentoring for Social Inclusion: A Critical Approach to Nurturing Mentor Relationships*. London: Routledge.

Daloz, J. (1986) *Effective Mentoring and Teaching*. San Francisco, CA: Jossey-Bass.

Habermas, J. (1989) *The Structural Transformation of the Public Sphere: An Inquiry into Bourgeois Society*. Cambridge, MA: MIT Press.

Hankey, J. (2004) The good, the bad and other considerations: reflections on mentoring trainee teachers in post-compulsory education, *Research in Post-Compulsory Education*, 9(3), 389–400.

Krippendorp, K. (2004) *Content Analysis: An Introduction to its Methodology*. Thousand Oaks, CA: Sage.

Lawy, R. and Tedder, M. (2011) Mentoring and individual learning plans: issues of practice in a period of transition, *Research in Post-Compulsory Education*, 16(3), 385–96.

Petty, G. (2009) *Teaching Today* (4th edn.). London: Hodder & Stoughton.

Rogers, C. (2004) *On Becoming a Person*. London: Constable.

Tedder, M. and Lawy, R. (2009) The pursuit of 'excellence': mentoring in further education initial teacher training in England, *Journal of Vocational Education and Training*, 61(4), 413–29.

Urban, M. (2008) Dealing with uncertainty: challenges and possibilities for the early childhood profession, *European Early Childhood Education Research Journal*, 16(2), 135–52.

Wolf, A. (2011) *Review of Vocational Education* (The Wolf Report). London: Department for Education/Department for Business, Innovation and Skills.

P

Part-time tutors
Pastoral care
Pedagogy
Personalised learning
Professional learning
Professionalism

Part-time tutors

The vast majority of tutors in adult and community education are employed on a part-time basis. Many further education colleges also employ tutors on a part-time basis. The position of part-time tutors in further and adult education continues to be an area of debate. Many tutors are employed on a termly or 'modular' basis (that is, they receive a contract for each module or group of modules that they will be teaching), with no guarantee of continuing employment during the following academic year. In the further education sector, it is the case that, for some tutors, part-time work can lead to a more permanent position, but in adult and community education full-time teaching roles are rare. It can be argued therefore that since the incorporation of further education colleges (following the 1992 Further and Higher Education Act), working conditions for part-time tutors in further education have been increasingly characterised by insecurity and 'casualisation'. For tutors in adult and community education, rather different conditions prevail: historically employment in this sector has always been predominantly part time and short term – that is, often taken up by people who neither want nor aspire to work full time for a variety of reasons. Nonetheless, insecurity of employment remains.

Part-time tutors occupy a variety of roles within an education or training organisation. Some part-timers workers, due to the nature of their post, will frequently be called upon to work with other members of staff, and despite their part-time status, will be fully integrated into the life and work of the organisation. It is common for part-time members of staff in a further education college to be wholly or partly responsible for admissions, for writing course evaluation reports, and for meeting external verifiers. For others, who perhaps teach only during the evening, opportunities for wider professional engagement are few. Demands such as these pose awkward questions for the part-time member of staff: a willingness to engage in duties outside the classroom or workshop may be looked upon favourably should a permanent position become available. However, it can be seen as unreasonable for colleges to demand that tutors who are in effect only paid according to the contact hours that they teach (and who will also need to prepare those sessions and mark the assignments that students produce) should also be required to undertake wider course management roles.

Adult education tutors working for a local education authority or for the Workers' Educational Association may have no professional responsibilities outside of the contact hours that they are paid to deliver. Indeed, they may be the only people tutoring their subject within that organisation, which can lead to a sense of professional isolation. For these tutors also, additional demands can be identified. Adult and community education is increasingly assessed and audited in the same way as a college course might be. Publicity and recruitment are areas of particular importance to these tutors. A term's employment will invariably rest upon successful recruitment to a course: if the number of students signing up to do a course is too low, the course will be cancelled.

At the same time, some of the wider professional demands that are placed on part-time tutors are equal to those required of full-time members of staff: part-time tutors are expected to undertake continuing professional development and to hold relevant professional qualifications. Here, too, complex arguments emerge. Students, quite rightly, expect the people who teach them to be appropriately qualified. But is it realistic or appropriate to expect that someone who only teaches for two or four hours a week should study for a CertEd/PGCE? Should part-time tutors – who are only paid for the hours that they teach – be required to attend training days that fall outside their normal patterns of employment? Conversations (at the time of writing) around the use of zero hours contracts in the public sector more generally have highlighted the insecurity that often characterises the part-time tutor's employment, and these are conversations that look set to continue in the near future.

Pastoral care

Pastoral care refers to the non-academic development of students. In 'faith' schools, a strong emphasis is placed upon the pastoral development of students. Their development as human beings is considered as important as their academic development. This connects with the critical pedagogy that is associated with the movement of emancipatory pedagogy. Instead of regarding students as consumers of education, Morley and Dunstan (2013) advocate resistance to this concept through the application of an emancipatory pedagogy that is based on the work of Freire (1973, 1985, 1994). Torres (1998, 2008) justifies this approach to teaching by citing examples of neoliberal educational reforms that are regarded as being essentially 'oppressive'. The critical pedagogy of Clegg *et al.* (2010), Morley and Dunstan (2013), and Torres (1998, 2008) apportions a developmental imperative to education. Moreover, Freire and Freire (1997: 80) argue that teaching should be based on a pedagogy in which 'all grow'.

Through dialogue, the-teacher-of-the-students and the student-of-the-teacher cease to exist and a new term emerges: teacher–student with student–teacher. The teacher is no longer the-one-who-teaches, but one who is him or herself taught in dialogue with the students, who in turn while being taught also teach. Far from being visualised as a 'tool' for teaching, pedagogy is interpreted by Freire (1997) as being a fundamental component of human nature and evidence that an educator has a democratic understanding of human society.

The work of Carl Rogers is also associated with pastoral care. Carl Rogers has had a particularly important influence on interpretations of the purpose of education. His work is also influential in what is considered as being effective pastoral care. One of the most important Rogerian ideas to have influenced education is the proposal that anxiety is a product of what has become termed the 'would/should dilemma'. This means that an individual wants to do something but they are unable to fulfil this wish. According to Rogers, this then generates tension within the individual, which, in turn, produces anxiety. In applying therapy to resolve the would/should dilemma, Rogers recommends that the therapist must have a 'congruent' or genuine interest in the person. Empathy is a central concept to the Rogerian model of client-centred therapy. The ideal aim is to lead the person being counselled to their 'inner beautiful self' so that the individual's would/should dilemma can be overcome.

It can be argued that there are merits in becoming aware of pastoral care. Students in the lifelong learning sector will at times need as much help and support as is possible. By becoming aware of these pastoral needs, the effectiveness of teaching and learning in the lifelong learning sector is likely to be enhanced. A raised awareness of pastoral care is also associated with other educational philosophies including the work of Steiner and Montessori. Both of these educationalists place an emphasis upon the importance of developing individuals as opposed to focusing upon academic achievement or 'the end product'.

Pedagogy

Pedagogy means the 'art' or 'science' or teaching. The term is often associated with younger rather than older learners (and the term andragogy). Effective pedagogy depends upon effective communication skills. The communication skills of the teacher become essential if creative and effective solutions to the challenges within the learning process are to be found. We need effective communication in pedagogy for a variety of reasons. We may need to modify behaviour by using verbal and non-verbal cues in order to achieve the required behavioural response. To ensure 'action' on the part of learners or 'persuade' them to do a learning activity, we will need particularly good communication skills. We need to apply communication skills in order to ensure that our learners understand what they are supposed to be doing. The most common forms of communication are the spoken word, the written word, visual images, and body language. Communication can be described as being the process of sending and receiving information. When communication between sender and receiver is poor, this might be due to 'distortion'.

It is not only what you say in the classroom that is important, but also how you say it that can make the difference to your learners. Non-verbal messages are an essential component of communication in the teaching process. Teachers should be aware of non-verbal behaviour in the classroom for three reasons:

1. Awareness of non-verbal behaviour allows you to become more aware of how your learners are communicating.
2. You will become a better communicator if you become aware of non-verbal messages.
3. This mode of communication increases the degree of the perceived psychological closeness between teacher and the learner.

Some major areas of non-verbal behaviours that influence pedagogy include:

- *Eye contact.* This is an important channel of interpersonal communication that helps in regulating the flow of communication. It signals interest in others. Eye contact with an audience increases the speaker's credibility. Teachers who make eye contact open the flow of communication and convey interest, concern, warmth and credibility.
- *Facial expressions.* Smiling is a powerful cue that transmits happiness, friendliness, warmth, liking and affection. If you smile frequently, you will be perceived as being more likeable, friendly, warm and approachable. Smiling is often contagious and students will react favourably and learn more.

- *Gestures.* If you fail to use gestures while speaking, you may be perceived as being 'unanimated' in your teaching. A lively and animated teaching style captures the learners' attention and makes the material more interesting. This can in turn facilitate learning and provide a bit of entertainment. 'Head nods' can also help in communicating positive reinforcement to the learners and indicate that you are listening to what they are saying.

- *Posture and body orientation.* We communicate numerous messages by the way we walk, talk, stand and sit. Standing erect, but not rigid, and leaning slightly forward communicates to the learners that you are approachable, respectful and friendly. Furthermore, interpersonal closeness results when you and your students face each other. Speaking with your back turned or looking at the floor or ceiling should be avoided. This can communicate disinterest to your learners.

- *Proximity.* Cultural norms dictate a comfortable distance for interaction with students. You should look for signals of discomfort caused by invading someone else's space. Some of these signs of discomfort include: rocking, leg swinging, tapping and aversion of gaze. To counteract this possibility, move around the classroom to increase interaction with your learners. Increasing proximity enables you to make better eye contact and increases the number of opportunities for the learners to speak.

- *Para-linguistics.* This aspect of non-verbal communication includes the vocal elements of tone, pitch, rhythm, timbre, loudness and inflection. For maximum teaching effectiveness, learn to vary these elements of your voice. If you speak to the learners in a 'monotone' voice, your style of teaching may be criticised. The students may learn less and consequently lose interest in learning.

- *Humour.* This aspect of pedagogy is sometimes overlooked as a teaching tool. Laughter releases stress and tension for both the teacher and the learners. It is important to develop an ability to laugh at yourself and encourage your learners to make sure that they are never too serious. This, in turn, fosters a friendly classroom environment that can help to facilitate learning.

- *Intelligence.* Not everyone can teach well! You need knowledge of your subject, as this will help to engender confidence. It is also important to ensure that you help to generate a facilitating atmosphere. To improve your non-verbal skills, you might want to videotape yourself speaking. You could then ask a colleague to suggest how you might change your style of delivery. You might also consider watching a recording of your teaching, as this can also help you to evaluate your non-verbal skills.

Personalised learning

Personalised learning means that the curriculum is adapted to the individual needs of the learner. This is increasingly important within the lifelong learning sector due to the diversity of our learners. An example of personalised learning can be seen in the humanist approaches to teaching and learning. There are a number of key principles that influence this idea of personalised learning.

The following key ideas are of particular importance in enabling personalised learning:

- allow students time to explore areas of curiosity;
- deliver teaching sessions that provide an intellectual challenge;
- plan and prepare lessons that connect areas of learning so that the learners are able to compare and contrast ideas;
- use an interactive approach to teaching whenever possible;
- enable the learners to approach topics of learning from as many various angles as possible;
- provide opportunities for philosophical thought and discussion where appropriate;
- involve the learners in learning activities that challenge their existing knowledge and understanding in an appropriate way.

Personalised learning is also associated with 'aesthetic learning'. Within the humanist pedagogy that enables personalised learning, importance is attached to developing the appreciation of human aesthetic qualities. This leads to an emphasis being placed on the following pedagogical aspects of the learning process.

1. Classroom materials ought to be arranged in a neat and 'easy on the eye' manner.
2. The learners' work ought to be displayed regularly if it shows the development and emergence of aesthetic qualities.
3. 'Colourful' and 'bright' displays reveal that learners are being enabled to apply their aesthetic abilities.
4. Learning materials ought to be updated so as to ensure that they do not become 'out of date'.
5. Teaching rooms need to be designed so that they create 'varied', 'appealing', and 'interesting' learning areas (for example, the main teaching room may be painted in colours that 'soften' the atmosphere such as 'light blue').
6. Large window areas let in light, which stimulates learning.

7.   Well-maintained physical surroundings (clean rooms, freshly painted walls, clean and maintained desks) can help to promote a positive learning environment.

The ultimate goal of personalised learning is to achieve 'self-actualisation'. This enables the learners to learn as independently as possible. This is at the heart of the meaning of the important humanist idea of 'self-actualisation'. Once learners become 'self-actualised', they are associated with the following attributes:

- the pedagogical process provides learners with the freedom to explore learning and discover on their own;
- learning becomes meaningful and connects 'real-life experiences';
- teaching sessions enable the learners to become involved in projects that help them to develop their powers of self-expression.

Humanists consider humans to be proactive unique individuals who exercise free will over their behaviour and emphasise the importance that 'choice' plays in enabling this ability to learn. The argument is developed that choice enables learners to engage with the learning process in an intense and personal way. Humanism emphasises the importance of drawing on experiences and interaction in order to develop critical thinking, initiative and self-directed learning. The humanist ideals for teaching and learning are appealing. Many of us enter the lifelong learning sector in order to facilitate learning so that the students experience change in a positive way. For this ideal of personalised learning to work, however, it is essential that the learners share the same values as their teachers. If this is not the case, it may be difficult to realise many of the profound values that this approach to teaching and learning stands for.

Professional learning

Courses and programmes of study that are linked both directly and indirectly to specific professions are a common feature of the curriculum in the lifelong learning sector. Courses relating to subject areas such as law, accountancy, veterinary nursing and teaching tend to be referred to collectively as 'professional learning'. Arguably this is something of a misleading term: the ways in which people learn during an accountancy course are no different from the ways in which people learn during a sociology course, but the latter would be defined as 'academic' rather than 'professional'. Similarly, 'learning' is the same irrespective of whether this learning is part of a teacher-training course or part of an engineering course. The term 'professional curriculum' is perhaps more accurate. The education of new teachers in further education colleges as they work towards CertEd/PGCE or DTLLS awards is an example of professional learning (although the extent to which such provision will survive in the new climate of voluntarism is yet to be seen).

Professional learning courses in further and adult education, irrespective of the exact topic(s) being followed, tend to share a number of characteristics:

- *Endorsement by a professional body.* A relevant professional body often endorses learning programmes such as these. Endorsement of this kind normally requires that the curriculum is mapped onto a series of professional standards or competences, and is in turn delivered to a set of standards or quality thresholds that are established by the professional body and monitored through a variety of inspection or audit processes.
- *Licence to practise.* One of the central foundations of any professional learning programme is that the successful completion of the programme awards the student a licence to practise – this might be an implicit aspect of certification, or an explicit public statement through the award of a professional status of some kind. However, it is also important to note that the level of professional competence thus established is at a threshold level – a level appropriate only for a new entrant to the profession. The assumption here is that the professional learning programme is not able to provide a thorough education in all of the skills, knowledge or attitudes that the profession requires. Instead, students will be equipped with the minimum necessary to enter the profession.
- *Continuing professional development* (CPD). Following the achievement of an initial or threshold level of professional competence, further professional learning is assumed to be a necessary element of ongoing professional practice. Many professions require members to complete a specified amount of CPD on an annual basis, through participating in activities that are often formally endorsed. The CPD requirements of the Institute for Learning, in contrast, are only loosely defined and endorsed (compared with other professions).
- *Authenticity in teaching, learning, and assessment.* Many professional learning courses require students either to be in relevant employment (on a full- or part-time basis), or to be able to access relevant unpaid or voluntary work experience, or to go on a placement. The alignment of authentic professional practice with teaching and learning strategies is also extended to assessment tasks, which often require the student to write about or reflect on workplace experiences. Assessment in professional learning courses is often referred to as 'high-stakes' assessment, as failure can in some cases lead to the student having to change career path.

Professional learning can also be seen happening in a less structured and more informal context. Researchers who have undertaken studies of informal learning at work have drawn attention to the ways in which informal groupings such as those found in staff rooms or at public events such as trade fairs or conferences can facilitate communication and learning between professionals. Indeed, in the case of teachers in further education colleges, it has been argued that informal episodes such as conversations in corridors or staffrooms are as important as formal programmes for promoting professional learning and development (Avis *et al.*, 2009).

Professionalism

Professionalism, strictly speaking, can be understood as consisting of the kinds of behaviour that are required from the members of a profession. But which kinds of occupation count as a profession, and which do not? Historically, some occupations have been classed as professions and others as vocations, but this is changing. Becoming a nurse used to be seen as a vocation, but is more often thought of as a profession these days; and it may not be a coincidence that as nursing has become a profession instead of a vocation, nurses are increasingly accessing higher education to gain appropriate qualifications. Originally, professions were seen as being distinct from vocations, and from other occupations that might be thought of as unskilled or not requiring mental or intellectual effort. Today, people still talk about the medical profession or the legal profession, but we would not describe a stonemason or an electrician as being members of a profession. However, it is quite possible that, having seen an electrician do a really good job when rewiring a house, he might be described as 'having done a really professional job'. And, just to add to the confusion, 'vocation' has also changed in meaning. In the lifelong learning sector, distinctions are often made between the academic curriculum and the vocational curriculum, the last referring to technical, manual or practical activity.

Briefly, and combining a number of different theoretical perspectives, a profession can be defined as possessing a number of characteristics, and one way of thinking about being a professional is the extent to which an occupation meets – or doesn't meet – the following six characteristics:

- a theoretical knowledge on which practical or skill-based activity rests;
- formal, accredited qualifications, awarded by an approved provider, which provide a grounding in the theoretical knowledge required;
- a licence to practise, or some other public proof of occupational competence, normally acquired by passing an examination;

- a code of professional conduct or practice;
- a professional body that represents the interests of practitioners, and regulates their activity in some way;
- some kind of concern as to the impact or consequences of the actions of members of the profession.

At first look, being a teacher in further or adult education clearly meets these characteristics. Practitioners study the theoretical basis of teaching and learning; they acquire teaching qualifications; they work towards QTLS; and they abide by codes of practice through the Institute for Learning (IfL). But recent moves (at the time of writing) towards voluntarism in obtaining teaching qualifications, speculation about the future of the IfL, and the uncertainty surrounding the role to be played by the Education and Training Foundation raises questions around how professionalism within the lifelong learning workforce is understood by policy makers. At best it would seem to be being neglected.

At the same time, other conversations about professionalism can be readily identified as having an impact on the daily working lives of teachers and trainers. Professionalism is contested within further and adult education, and is seen as being imposed on the workforce, reducing professional autonomy and increasing forms of managerial control. Within this model, professionals need to be constantly observed to ensure that targets are met and accountability is established. These discourses of professionalism are seen as being rooted in (although not solely caused by) the incorporation of further education colleges over twenty years ago, which brought with it new and aggressive forms of management and significant deterioration of working conditions. Teachers in adult education have faced similarly precarious conditions of employment since the mid-1990s, following a series of cuts to funding provision and the introduction of compulsory assessment for all forms of adult education provision that might attract government funding. In this context, professionalism is understood in terms of requiring compliance and flexibility and being critical of working practices is seen as 'unprofessionalism'. Clearly, the meaning of professionalism within the lifelong learning sector will continue to be contested.

References and further reading

Alcock, C., Payne, S. and Sullivan, M. (2000) *Introducing Social Policy*. Harlow: Prentice-Hall.

Avis, J., Orr, K. and Tummons, J. (2009) Theorising the work-based learning of teachers, in J. Avis, R. Fisher and R. Thompson (eds.) *Teaching in Lifelong Learning: A Guide to Theory and Practice*. Maidenhead: McGraw-Hill.

Cameron, D. (2009) *Party Leader's address*. Speech to Conservative Party Conference, 8 October, Manchester.

Clegg, S., Hudson, A. and Steel, J. (2010) The emperor's new clothes: globalisation and e-learning in higher education, *British Journal of Sociology of Education*, 24(1), 39–53.

Duckworth, V. and Tummons, J. (2010) *Contemporary Issues in Lifelong Learning*. Maidenhead: McGraw-Hill/Open University Press.

Freire, P. (1973) *Education for Critical Consciousness*. New York: Seabury Press.

Freire, P. (1985) *The Politics of Education: Culture, Power and Liberation*. South Hadley, MA: Bergin & Garvey.

Freire, P. (1994) *Pedagogy of Hope: Reliving the Pedagogy of the Oppressed*. New York: Continuum.

Freire, P. and Freire, A.M.A. (1997) *Pedagogy of the Heart*. New York: Continuum.

Gleeson, D., Davies, J. and Wheeler, E. (2005) On the making and taking of professionalism in the further education workplace, *British Journal of Sociology of Education*, 26(4), 445–60.

Harris, B. (2004) *The Origins of the British Welfare State*. Basingstoke: Palgrave Macmillan.

Morley, C. and Dunstan, J. (2013) A response to neoliberal challenges to field education, *Social Work Education*, 32(2), 141–56.

Selwyn, N. (2011) The place of technology in the Conservative–Liberal Democrat education agenda: an ambition of absence?, *Educational Review*, 63(4), 395–408.

Torres, C.A. (1998) *Democracy, Education and Multiculturalism*. Lanham, MD: Rowman & Littlefield.

Torres, C.A. (2008) *Education and Neoliberal Globalisation*. New York: Taylor & Francis.

Tummons, J. (2010) *Becoming a Professional Tutor in the Lifelong Learning Sector* (2nd edn.). Exeter: Learning Matters.

Weardon, G. (2010) Shares in Promethean tumble as education austerity measures bite, *The Guardian*, 24 August.

Q

Qualifications

Quality assurance

Qualifications

Achieving a qualification is, in essence, a way for a student to be able to demonstrate publicly that she or he has successfully learned whatever the course in question was about, through having been awarded a document – a certificate of some kind – that can be used to provide quick and convenient evidence of having done so. Qualifications are warrants of achievement, of having learned a series of technical skills, of having demonstrated the required level of occupational competence, or of having mastered a body of academic knowledge. Their importance rests in what they permit the student to do. Qualifications – at whatever level and in whatever subject – are required by students for two main reasons: first, to allow the student to enter or move within the world of work; and second, to allow the student to access a higher level of education or training provision. At the same time, the qualification process allows institutions to demonstrate the effectiveness of their education and training provision through making results public (in league tables, or as part of an Ofsted report). An almost bewildering array of qualifications is offered within the lifelong learning sector notwithstanding efforts, following recommendations made in the Wolf Report (2011), to reduce their number. In many areas of the curriculum, qualifications are offered by more than one awarding body. This can lead to institutional decisions to offer awards from one body rather than another for administrative or financial, as well as academic or curricular, reasons.

The grading and awarding of qualifications is subject to a significant amount of coverage by the media – a situation that, arguably, has been exacerbated by successive governmental changes to curriculum, organisation, and funding within the further and adult education sectors. Debates (which are more or less well informed) around 'grade inflation' and 'dumbing-down' at GCSE and A level have parallels within the lifelong learning sector in debates around the lack of 'value' or 'worth' of some qualifications in the eyes of employers (an issue that was discussed at length in the Wolf Report, 2011). These debates can be located within the wider shift during the last 30 years to a mass education system – that is, an education system that sets out to provide study routes, curricula, and qualifications for a majority, rather than a minority, of the population. Put simply, qualifications can be obtained, at the current time, in subject areas that were not accredited and certified 20 or 30 years ago. In part, this is due to shifts in the curriculum over time – the rapid growth of ICT being an obvious example. But this is also due in part to conscious decisions taken by policy makers to expand formal curricular provision within colleges and adult education centres into areas that historically were only represented within informal and/or work-based settings. Several issues are at work here. There is the ongoing debate around how parity ought to be achieved between academic and vocational curricula (the conversion of the polytechnics into universities in 1992 being one effect of this debate), which forms one reason for the growth in provision of qualifications in 'non-academic' subject areas. The need to prevent too many young people from entering the workforce is another. And discourses of *widening participation* can also be discerned in discussions regarding the provision of new forms of curriculum in order to encourage more young people (at whom such policies are invariably targeted) to remain in education and training. One of the more strident criticisms of *vocationalism* was that of Bernstein (1990), who argued that the vocational curriculum in general (here understood to include all of the courses and qualifications that are available) and the ways in which policy makers stress the value of vocational programmes and awards, in fact serve to restrict rather than widen opportunity, because they are only ever targeted at a particular sector of the population – the 'working class' – who would be doing those kinds of course anyway.

Quality assurance

Quality assurance encompasses a range of activities by a number of different stakeholders, all of which are directed to the evaluation of a particular process or practice. In the context of the lifelong learning sector, quality assurance systems can be understood as being concerned with the quality of the specific education or training provision that is under review, where 'quality' is understood as relating to the quality of teaching provision, of resources, of assessment processes, of management and administrative support, and so forth. The quality assurance of education and training provision can therefore be seen as concerned with all aspects of curricular delivery. The outputs of quality assurance systems are similarly varied. To be found alongside well-known and public processes such as Ofsted inspections are parallel quality assurance processes that are conducted within organisations: observations of teaching and learning are a common feature of working life within the lifelong learning sector. Awarding and professional bodies manage their own quality assurance through processes such as external validation and verification (the processes by which providers are initially endorsed and subsequently monitored in the delivery of a particular curriculum).

Quality assurance (QA) processes speak to a number of different stake-holders in the lifelong learning sector. As well as being able to assure students that the courses that they are choosing to follow are appropriately resourced, planned, and delivered, QA also serves to address the concerns of: funding bodies and relevant government departments; employers and employers' bodies such as Sector Skills Councils (which are involved in the establishment of occupational standards and hence in the design of the curriculum); and the parents of students attending further education colleges.

The arguments that invariably surround the Ofsted inspection process notwithstanding, the broader phenomenon of QA is far from uncontroversial. Quality assurance is seen as being wrapped up in what are termed 'audit cultures': workplace cultures that are characterised by systems for evaluating or measuring the activities or practices that take place within them. Audit cultures within education (and by extension within the public sector more generally) have expanded significantly during the last 20 to 30 years, and are seen as accompanying a shift towards the application of 'free market' or 'private sector' working methods and cultures to the public sector. Audit cultures are associated with two aspects of organisational or workplace culture and practice. The first of these is *managerialism*, defined as an ethos of management within an organisation where such management helps the organisation in question to be as productive as it can possibly be. The second of these is *performativity*, which is defined as a culture of workplace organisation where management imposes systems based around targets and judgements, against which both organisations (further education colleges or adult education providers) and individuals (teachers and trainers) are evaluated.

Criticisms of audit cultures within the lifelong learning sector (remembering that parallel criticisms can be found in other organisational contexts such as the National Health Service in the UK) tend to revolve around the impact of such cultures on working practices and workplace culture (which are seen as being damaged by quality assurance practices), on relationships between managers and teachers or trainers (which are seen as being confrontational rather than cooperative in nature), and on concepts of *professionalism*. While there are no serious proposals to dismantle quality assurance processes in their entirety, arguments have been made that they should be scaled back both in terms of the resources involved (quality assurance and inspection regimes are time consuming, bureaucratic, and costly) and in terms of what kinds of activity ought to come under their purview.

References and further reading

Bernstein, B. (1990) *Class Codes and Control IV: The Structuring of Pedagogic Discourse.* London: Routledge.

Hayes, D., Marshall, T. and Turner, A. (eds.) (2007) *A Lecturer's Guide to Further Education.* Maidenhead: McGraw-Hill.

Hilborne, J. (1996) Ensuring quality in further and higher education partnerships, in M. Abramson, J. Bird and A. Stennett (eds.) *Further and Higher Education Partnerships: The Future for Collaboration.* Buckingham: Open University Press/ Society for Research into Higher Education.

Marsden, F. and Youde, A. (2010) Administration and course management, in J. Avis, R. Fisher and R. Thompson (eds.) *Teaching in Lifelong Learning: A Guide to Theory and Practice.* Maidenhead: McGraw-Hill.

Tummons, J. (2011) Actors, networks and assessment: an actor–network critique of quality assurance in higher education in England, in A. Tatnall (ed.) *Actor–Network Theory and Technology Innovation: Advancements and New Concepts.* Hershey, PA: IGI Global.

Wolf, A. (2011) *Review of Vocational Education* (The Wolf Report). London: Department for Education/Department for Business, Innovation and Skills.

R

Recreational learning
Reflective practice
Research
Resources

Recreational learning

Recreational learning is often associated with community education – the education takes place in community colleges, libraries, and other locations (including people's homes). Part-time programmes with a basis in cultural interests, including languages, art classes, sports and cooking classes, make up some of the recreational education within the lifelong learning sector.

The following key ideas are of particular importance in recreational learning:

- Recreational education is about enjoying learning.
- Recreational education is not about acquiring qualifications.
- A particular sort of teaching approach occurs in recreational learning. The social side of learning may enable the development of a humanist style of teaching and learning.
- Learners are provided with opportunities for creative development where appropriate.
- Learners are involved in in learning activities in order to generate feelings of pleasure and satisfaction.

Recreational learning is based on developing 'self-esteem' within the learning process. A number of key aspects of pedagogy can help in developing learners' self-esteem so that the learners engage with the learning process. It is important to ensure that the development of new knowledge is based on what has been previously learned, to help facilitate the development of the 'scaffolding' process of learning. It is also vital to:

- focus on the learning strengths of the learners and their key learning abilities;
- take individual needs and abilities into account when planning lessons and carrying them out;
- teach and model helpful learning strategies for the learners (for example, by making sure that you are able to demonstrate what the learners are expected to do when they are learning);
- base new teaching, strategies and plans on manageable learning outcomes;
- be alert to learners' difficulties with the learning process so that you can intervene and help as soon as possible;
- be available and approachable so that those learners having difficulties with learning feel comfortable and able to 'ask for help';
- involve all the learners in classroom activities;
- apply discipline as appropriately as possible;
- gain respect from others in order to develop a learning environment where the learners are 'positive' as opposed to being 'judgemental';
- provide rewards for completing work well;
- develop and apply a curriculum that enables learners to become empathetic and sociable learners;
- apply cooperative learning in such a way as to develop trust between learners;
- involve learners in activities that they see as being 'important' and 'worthwhile'.

Once again, 'softer skills' seem to be required by those working in recreational education. The tension that exists with recreational learning is that it is a form of learning that is different to the 'target-driven' curriculum that Lucas (2007) writes about. This means that recreational learning may be seen to be at odds with the accepted ideas of the purpose of education. The message from successive governments is that qualifications and meeting targets are all that matters within the education system. The idea of 'education for fun' or education for 'communitarian values' is seen by many to be at odds with this value. The lifelong learning sector might be able to learn from other countries, such as Sweden, and their approach to education. Instead of a process of audit and an emphasis placed on obtaining qualifications, the Swedish system is much more supportive of education that is neither measured nor assessed. This represents the ideals of recreational education. Who is to say that this form of education is in any way an inferior part of what happens in the lifelong learning sector?

Reflective practice

Reflective practice is a process of critical introspection and self-evaluation leading, it has been argued, to the development of professional knowledge. The key theoretical elements of reflective practice can be found in the writing of a small number of key thinkers:

John Dewey

Dewey argued that when encountering a problem, teachers engage in a process of reflective thinking, leading to learning that would allow a solution to be found. In fact, reflective thinking can only happen in these circumstances. Dewey proposed a five-stage model of problem solving: suggestions (possible solutions to the problem that has been encountered are considered); intellectualisation (questions are advanced); hypothesis formation (the teacher starts to put together a number of possible solutions); reasoning (the solution that has been settled on is carefully thought about); testing (the solution to the problem is tested out in the real world).

Donald Schön

Donald Schön proposed two forms of reflective practice: reflection-in-action and reflection-on-action. *Reflection-in-action* is an instantaneous process, triggered immediately as the teacher solves a problem or encounters a dilemma during teaching. Reflection-in-action is found in that moment when the teacher, drawing on their experience, knowledge, skills, and understanding of this and other situations changes direction and decides to run the session differently, or to change the planned sequence of activities for that session, or to introduce something new. *Reflection-on-action* is a more deliberative process. When reflecting on action, the teacher needs to think critically about what has taken place, to analyse and evaluate the actions that were carried out, and to consider what might have happened if a different course of action had been chosen.

Stephen Brookfield

Stephen Brookfield proposed a model for reflective practice that rested on four perspectives – that of the practitioner; the students; the practitioner's colleagues; and established theory. The unpacking of assumptions such as 'student-led methods are always superior to teacher-led methods' is what characterises critical reflection according to Brookfield. For example, a teacher working in adult education might, quite understandably, be committed to a student-centred approach to learning. From the point of view of the teacher, such student-led activities empower the students, encourage them to take responsibility for their own learning, and promote a facilitative approach in which the students learn from one another, as well as from the teacher. However, some students may require a more structured, teacher-led pedagogy, and may not be ready for independent learning.

Aspects of both the theory and application of reflective practice have been subjected to exploration and criticism by a range of researchers and writers (Ecclestone, 1996; Jarvis, 2010; Tummons, 2011):

1. Many versions of reflective practice are currently advocated in the literature, but despite this proliferation of writing, the nature of the reflective process itself continues to elude us.
2. In the many writings on reflective practice, the ways by which professional learning or knowledge are encouraged or created remain obscure. This is problematic because the development of knowledge is positioned as a key benefit of the process.
3. Reflective practice cannot be assessed because it is, simply put, impossible to assess – something that cannot be properly described or defined. Reflective practice is such a troublesome concept that it cannot be summarised in outcomes/objectives.
4. The formal, structured format of reflective practice that is presented during periods of initial professional development stands in stark contrast to the messy reality of the lifelong learning sector workplace. The prompts to reflective practice that are invariably embedded in assignment tasks and individual learning plans have no equivalent in the working lives of teachers who work in a complex environment.

Research

Research is an important part of every academic discipline. The term 'research' means discovering new information about a subject. When we discover this new information, it enables us to confirm or dispute whether previous understandings of academic matters still apply. Two especially influential theories have influenced research: the 'positivist' and 'interpretive' models of research. The two theoretical perspectives provide opposing models of research. The positivist perspective is scientific in its approach. This is because it recommends that the best way to gather research data is to adopt a scientific perspective in order to gather statistics and quantifiable data. In contrast, the interpretive perspective is non-scientific in its approach. Interpretive research attempts to gather the views and opinions of individuals in a non-statistical way. These narrative accounts are used to present individual interpretations of the social world. Both approaches to research are summarised in the following definition of research:

> 1. diligent and systematic inquiry or investigation into a subject in order to revise facts, theories, applications, etc. (*Random House Dictionary of the English Language*, 1987)

Research is important for the lifelong learning sector because it provides the opportunity to revise and reinforce understandings of teaching and learning. Becoming aware of the research process enables you to increase your knowledge of the latest findings about the factors influencing the lifelong learning sector.

The research process is characterised by competing models of research. Above we refer to the positivist and interpretive models of research. Both of these paradigms have their own distinctive philosophy of the research process. In other words, the data-gathering methods that are chosen are influenced by the underlying research philosophy. Whereas the positivist approach to research emphasises the importance of 'scientific processes', the interpretive perspective is non-scientific in its outlook. This results in data-gathering methods that are concerned with gathering non-scientific or qualitative data.

As well as the positivist and interpretive research perspectives, 'action research' is another influential research perspective. This research model emphasises the importance of researching professional practice so that the findings can be used to influence future work. This approach to research is often used within education so that the findings can be applied to improve professional practice. These research perspectives are described as being in competition because they have conflicting understandings of the research process and how this process should be applied.

Research methods refer to the data-collection processes that are applied by researchers. The data that are gathered are in general either 'quantitative' (or statistical) or 'qualitative' (or non-statistical). The research methods employed by the researcher are either 'primary' (or the immediate work of the researcher) or 'secondary' (i.e. using the findings of other published researchers). The techniques used to gather these data can include questionnaires, interviews, observations, focus groups, case studies and book-based research in 'learning resource centres'.

Researchers need to be aware of ethical good practice. Ethics refers to applying moral principles in order to ensure that the research process does not put the participants at harm. Opie (2004: 25) defines research ethics as 'the application of moral principles to prevent harming or wronging others, to promote the good, to be respectful and fair'. Ethics needs to be considered at all points of the study, from the design of the research question to interpreting the results and presenting the findings.

Resources

Advice and guidance regarding the design, use and evaluation of resources for teaching and learning is a common feature of teacher-training programmes across all education sectors in the UK. The use of different resources in the seminar room or workshop is an important element of the teaching and learning process. If they are chosen and used carefully, they can offer additional forms of information, engagement and motivation. This can be seen as working in a number of ways:

- Resources can supplement another teaching and learning strategy. For example, a handout can provide reinforcement for a topic that if only discussed verbally, might be too complex for some students to understand at first. Showing diagrams or photographs on a screen at the front of the seminar room can similarly reinforce the teaching of any number of topics.
- 'Real-world' resources add a further level of engagement. More importantly, they add authenticity to the teaching and learning process. Engineering workshops and art studios are both excellent examples of teaching and learning environments that rely on real-world tools, resources or equipment.
- If 'real-world' resources are unavailable (for reasons of space or cost), the creative use of resources can act as a substitute, to bring the real world of whatever curriculum is being followed 'into the classroom'. The increasing ubiquity of information and communication technologies (ICTs) makes the use of video and audio straightforward to plan and implement.

However, resources are also sometimes used at random and with insufficient planning and preparation. In these circumstances, they can have a negative rather than positive effect, acting as a distraction to teaching and learning:

- Handouts or PowerPoint presentations that are overloaded with text, an excessive number of images or (in the case of PowerPoint) needless animation effects, distract rather than aid students.
- Resources that contain spelling mistakes or incorrect grammar are a distraction and fail to support the literacy learning of students. They should always be corrected if a mistake is found. If a mistake is only noticed in the workshop or seminar room, then a corrected version should be distributed as soon as possible.
- If the teacher or trainer is not familiar or comfortable with the resource to be used, then it should be put to one side. For this reason, borrowing materials from colleagues is best avoided unless the teacher knows

exactly how it should be used – this might relate to something as simple as a handout or as complex as a computer application.

While staff working in further education colleges usually have more-or-less ready access to the materials that they need for creating resources, tutors working in adult education and lifelong learning often find themselves working in more constrained environments. They may have to use their own materials, tools, desktop computers and printers, since they often do not have access to a staff room or other institutional space, and (although this is by no means a given) claim additional expenses to compensate them for the materials that they have had to purchase. For hourly-paid tutors, the time spent creating resources can be considerable and may not be properly recognised. In contexts such as these, tutors should be mindful of the balance between needing to prepare appropriate materials for their classes and not spending so long in preparing them that their remuneration is inadequate.

Teachers and trainers need to ensure that their resources work alongside their own careful planning, their own extensive subject knowledge, and their own enthusiasm and motivation. A technically brilliant PowerPoint presentation embedded with images, hyperlinks and sounds is no substitute for a well-informed and enthusiastic teacher who understands how to motivate her or his students, how to use question-and-answer techniques properly, and how to give appropriate and constructive feedback as part of the formative assessment process.

References and further reading

Bryman, A. (2012) *Social Research Methods* (4th edn.). Oxford: Oxford University Press.

Ecclestone, K. (1996) The reflective practitioner: mantra or a model for emancipation?, *Studies in the Education of Adults*, 28(2), 146–62.

Jarvis, P. (2010) *Adult Education and Lifelong Learning: Theory and Practice* (4th edn.). London: Routledge.

Lucas, N. (2007) The in-service training of adult literacy, numeracy and English for Speakers of Other Languages teachers in England: the challenges of a 'standards-led model, *Journal of In-Service Education*, 33(1), 125–42.

Opie, C. (2004) *Doing Educational Research: A Guide to First Time Researchers*. London: Sage.

Random House (1987) *Random House Dictionary of the English Language* (2nd edn., unabridged). New York: Random House.

Rogers, C. (2004) *On Becoming a Person*. London: Constable.

Tummons, J. (2011) 'It sort of feels uncomfortable': problematising the assessment of reflective practice, *Studies in Higher Education*, 36(4), 471–83.

Tummons, J. and Duckworth, V. (2012) *Doing Your Research Project in the Lifelong Learning Sector*. Maidenhead: McGraw-Hill.

S

Safeguarding
Schemes of work
Self-directed learning
Skills
Social learning theory
Social policy
Syllabus

Safeguarding

Safeguarding is associated with the protection of young people. In the UK, the word 'safeguarding' has become synonymous with cases of abuse of children and young people. There have been a number of cases (for example, the case of 'Baby Peter') where children and young people appear to have been let down by those who ought to have been responsible for ensuring their welfare. Safeguarding policies are likely to impact upon your role in the lifelong learning sector. It is important to ensure that the young people you are educating are kept as safe as possible. Risk assessment forms need to be completed if you are taking a group of young people on an outing. A particular ratio of staff to learners is necessary in order to reduce as much as possible any risk developing. It is necessary to be vigilant in situations where abusive relations may be present. A student may exhibit signs of being abused and this may require intervention from health and social care professionals.

The policy approach that has been favoured in the UK in recent years has encouraged partnership and multi-agency working between health, care, and education organisations. Giddens (2004) argues that the concept of 'partnership' has characterised recent government approaches to safeguarding. All the sectors of the 'mixed economy of care' (statutory, private, voluntary, and informal) are encouraged to work together. This inter-agency approach to providing what former Prime Minister Tony Blair referred to as *joined-up solutions to joined-up problems* has been continued in the UK by the Coalition government. One of the main features of New Labour that is associated with safeguarding is 'Every Child Matters'.

Every Child Matters was published in 2004. The legislation resulted from the inquiry into the death of Victoria Climbié. *Every Child Matters: Change for Children* (DfES, 2004) represents the government's formal attempt to ensure that 'children aged 0 to 19' are 'protected' or 'safeguarded'. Every Child Matters has five main aims. The legislation reveals the government's commitment to ensuring that every child in the UK is 'healthy, safe, enjoys life and achieves/ makes a positive social contribution, and achieves economic well-being'. The key theme of the legislation is that the five main legislative aims can be achieved if 'integrated services for children' are ensured. This key point emphasises the importance of statutory, private, voluntary, and informal agencies working together through partnership. The cooperation between 'local and central children's services' is also seen as being an integral component of 'effective children's services'. This process involves 'planning, implementing and assessing the effectiveness of children's services'.

Every Child Matters was an example of a New Labour policy that attempted to improve the quality of life of children and families by ensuring safeguarding. It can be argued that this is in itself a worthwhile aim. Lumsden (2005) argues that the partnership approach with its emphasis on 'collaboration' does facilitate a model of 'coming together to solve problems' by providing integrated services. It can be argued that a weakness of Every Child Matters rests within its over-ambitious aims. The challenge with safeguarding is the complex nature of child abuse cases. This may mean that it is impossible to ensure that every child in the UK is 'healthy, safe, enjoys life and achieves, makes a positive social contribution, and achieves economic well-being'.

Schemes of work

Schemes of work are documents that outline the learning that will occur over a programme of study. They are different to lesson plans because lesson plans outline what will occur within individual teaching sessions. Teachers and students use a scheme of work for reference. It is generally accepted that it is good practice to give the students a scheme of work at the beginning of the academic year. This scheme of work outlines what will be studied and when. The scheme of work identifies when the programme assessments are due to be submitted. The other advantage of a scheme of work is that it is a useful document for other tutors who may be associated with your module. The scheme of work can help these tutors to see what needs to be covered in the teaching sessions. Most teachers in the lifelong learning sector would probably agree that schemes of work are helpful ways of planning and managing the academic year. A scheme of work may also be a highly useful resource for students who are able to identify from the first teaching session what will happen during the subsequent academic year.

Rogers (2004) emphasises the importance of ensuring that learners are made to feel as comfortable as possible during the learning process. If students are anxious about what they are expected to study or if they are unsure about what they are expected to do for their programme assessments, this can lead to what Rogers (2004) refers to as a 'would/should dilemma'. The students are unable to identify what they have to do in their programme of study and this generates anxiety and uncertainty. Rogers (2004) acknowledges that a means of resolving this tension is through the provision of a scheme of work at the beginning of the teaching year that identifies the content to be covered.

Schemes of work are also associated with controversy. A document that outlines the teaching topics and the forms of assessment alongside the helpful resources that are to be used is useful and shows good organisation. The influence of Ofsted, however, alongside its resulting curriculum developments, has had consequences for schemes of work. The detail that is required in a scheme of work by the Inspectorate is considerable. As opposed to being a document that outlines teaching sessions and assessments and resource, all sorts of other elements appear to be required by Ofsted. In a recent inspection of initial teacher training, the scheme of work was required to show where 'subject specialist' knowledge was being taught. The scheme of work was also expected to demonstrate where functional skills of maths, English, and ICTs appeared. This complicated example appeared to be a deviation from the original purpose of a scheme of work. Pleasing the Inspectorate appeared to be the primary focus for this scheme of work.

It is important to ensure that schemes of work are being used for teaching and learning purposes. If they are 'driven' by the Ofsted inspection process, the scheme of work can appear to be more of an element of bureaucracy. This represents a deviation from the original intention of a scheme of work. It sounds more akin to entering the 'bureaucratic cage' Weber (1983) has written – and warned us – about.

Self-directed learning

Although the term 'self-directed' might be attached to the exploration of much *formal* and/or *informal learning*, here 'self-directed learning' refers to the provision of education and training courses that do not rely on formal pedagogy as delivered by a teacher or trainer who stands at the front of a workshop or walks around a seminar room. Instead, the courses are based on a pedagogy that is delivered through the use of structured tasks in workbooks or webpages, sometimes with a tutor occupying a facilitative or trouble-shooting role in the background, but primarily designed so that the student works through a series of activities which are then checked or assessed (either through online testing or through the appraisal of a tutor) before the student can move on to the next stage of the programme of study. Thus, for example, while the learning that takes place when a student who attends a further education college sits down at home to do some reading can be seen as self-directed, it is to the particular curricular provision of 'resource-led' self-directed learning that we refer to here.

The most successful – and certainly the most well known in a UK context – example of self-directed learning provision is that of the Open University. While maintaining a large campus that is home to a number of faculties and research students, the vast majority of the Open University's provision at undergraduate and postgraduate level rests on a distance learning model that can be seen as self-directed. Although tutors are attached to modules and are able to offer additional support (historically, this was done through telephone or postal correspondence; tutors now use email and a virtual learning environment), the 'teaching' of a module is conducted through a course handbook. A similar approach to course resources has been adopted in so-called 'open learning' sessions run by further education colleges or local education authorities, and in the online provision offered by learndirect (publicly funded, but since 2011 a private training provider).

A typical handbook, or on-screen environment, for a self-directed learning course consists of a number of elements, typically including: a series of step-by-step instructions to guide the student from activity to activity or topic to topic; small exercises designed to reinforce learning that has already taken place; explanatory or expository text that provides information or knowledge for the student; and references or links to other materials that the student will be required to read or otherwise familiarise themselves with. In essence, such handbooks provide the instructional or pedagogical element of the programme, whether being delivered at a distance or in a community education building with a tutor – in a 'facilitator' role – available for questions and help.

Advocates of self-directed learning point to the flexibility and affordability of such provision as being significant factors in driving demand. And it remains the case that for many students, the ability to reconcile work, family and other commitments with flexible learning programmes such as these is attractive. However, critics point to the relatively high attrition rates that characterise such provision (a concern that is once again being voiced, currently in relation to massive open online courses). Another criticism of such provision has centred on the diminished role of the teacher or trainer: in many further and adult education institutions, staff facilitating 'open learning' programmes such as these are invariably paid at a lower rate than those who are 'teaching' face-to-face classes, even though one-to-one support is often required. It is undoubtedly the case that in some contexts cost rather than pedagogic factors have driven provision. When done well – which involves a considerable amount of preparatory work – such provision can be of high quality and of high value to the student.

Skills

A brief look at ways in which the word 'skill' is used within the further education and lifelong learning sectors quickly indicates a variety of meanings, usually depending on context. Common usage of the work implies some expertise in an activity developed as the result of training and/or experience, which has enabled the learner to carry out particular tasks. In this sense, the word 'skill' is usually defined in terms of an ability to carry out consistently a particular task towards a particular goal or end process, with accuracy, speed and economy of action; as an ability, which has been learned, to perform a complex task involving physical coordination with ease, speed and accuracy (a definition that foregrounds the academic/vocational divide that is a common feature of the further education and lifelong learning sectors), which has been built up gradually in the course of repeated training or other experience.

Over recent years, however, the meanings of 'skill' have changed and moved. This is indicated by the gradual introduction of expressions such as 'transferable skills' and 'employability skills'. These concepts remove the word 'skill' from a specific, contextualised meaning – that is, when skills are attached to or associated with specific crafts or trades, for example, or when they are attached to particular mental processes through expressions such as 'cognitive skills' or 'study skills' – and move it to a more general discussion about the learning that takes place in further education colleges or adult education centres. This more general discussion, which is partly informed by changes in political and economic pressures, has led to a number of expressions that include:

- *Functional skills* – the practical skills in English, ICT, and mathematics that allow individuals to work confidently, effectively, and independently in life. Reflecting changes in policy, these have also been known as 'key skills' and 'core skills' in recent years.
- *Study skills* – the transferable skills such as 'note taking' and 'critical thinking' that are important for students to acquire if they are going to be successful in their chosen programme of study.
- *Employability skills* –skills that are positioned, by employers, as necessary attributes for successful employment, such as 'team working skills' and 'time management skills'.

The ways in which 'skill' is used in the examples above are quite different to the 'common usage' definitions already provided. The 'common usage' definition places 'a skill' as a specific attribute or competence that, once practised

and acquired, would allow the student to perform a particular action or proce-
dure as part of a programme of learning within a specific area (for example,
electrical installation, millinery or hairdressing). But the definition of 'skills'
that is suggested by phrases such as 'functional skills' or 'study skills' is more
generic, seeing skills as something that can be acquired in a variety of ways
and applied to different employment or educational contexts. In this sense, a
'skill' is not a discrete quality that is situated within a specific context, but a
transferable quality that can travel from one context to another.

At the same time, 'skills' have become an object for policy analysis and
intervention, and this is reflected in other usages of the term. Further education
colleges as well as adult education providers such as the Workers' Educational
Association are funded by the Skills Funding Agency, which in turn reports to
the Department for Business, Innovation and Skills (BIS). Policy makers talk
about a 'skills gap' or a 'skills deficit' and employees are exhorted to 'up-skill'
or 're-skill' in order to maximise their chances of future employment, while
employers complain that college leavers lack the skills that they need to enter
the job market. However they are defined and whatever context they are found
in, 'skills' are of wider political, as well as individual, importance.

Social learning theory

Social learning theory is a term used to describe a number of different theories of learning that are based on long-term anthropological and ethnographic
research, in contrast to theories such as neo-behaviourism or constructivism,
which derive from psychology. Anthropology is the study of human societies
and relations, including how and why people live in the ways that they do,
how societies are organised, how cultures reproduce themselves, and so forth.
Ethnography is the study of cultures and societies from within, on their own
terms. From this perspective, the problems with psychological approaches are:

- The research done by psychologists and the conclusions that they
  draw are assumed to be straightforwardly transferable from laboratory settings to the outside world. Similarly, what people learn is
  assumed to be straightforwardly transferable from one setting to
  another.
- Psychological theories shape both educational theories and educational practices. The psychologists' focus on cognition foregrounds
  intellectual work at the expense of other kinds of learning, such as
  learning a craft.
- The knowledge that is said to be contained within formal academic
  curricula is assumed to have a higher status than the 'everyday'
  knowledge of peoples' family or working lives.

For practitioners who are interested in how and why people learn, how people are taught things, and what kinds of knowledge or ability are valued within societies, a social learning approach raises a number of interesting issues:

- The kinds of knowledge that are valued in particular settings are very variable, and depend on that setting. It is not the case that some kinds of knowledge are 'better' than others (for example, in the way that the academic curriculum in the UK is perceived as being superior to the vocational curriculum).
- If it is accepted that knowledge is specific and linked to the setting or context in which it is found or used, ideas about the transfer of learning need to be reconsidered.
- There is more to knowing things than simply having lots of qualifications. The things that people know can be seen in how they work, how they live with their families and friends, how they go about all kinds of activities in work and at leisure.

Social learning theory (examples include *activity theory* and *communities of practice*) is under-represented in teacher-training courses, which tend to focus on just a small number of psychological approaches, although this is now changing. One recent research project that has explored learning and teaching within further education was the Transforming Learning Cultures Project, which ran from 2001 to 2005 and was based on a case-study approach of teaching and learning at 19 different sites across four further education colleges. The main findings were:

1. Learning in further education colleges is shaped by complex cultural relationships.
2. What counts as good teaching varies across different institutional contexts, and across different subject areas.
3. Learning outcomes are numerous, and are highly variable. They are not always entirely beneficial to the student. For example, nursery nurses achieve a qualification and become practitioners, but are as a result identified as low-status and low-paid workers by the wider labour market.
4. Learning in further education is being damaged by unstable and inadequate funding regimes and by an over-emphasis (driven by audit and inspection cultures) on measuable learning outcomes.
5. For learning in further education to improve, the sector needs to receive sufficient funding on a more stable basis, more consistent and less rapidly chaning policy objectives, and enhanced staff professionalism.

6. A greater range of learning outcomes (including those articulated by students) should be recognised.
7. There should be a move towards greater professional autonomy and expertise for practitioners in the sector.

Social policy

Alcock *et al.* (2000: 1) define social policy as being 'the practical application and implementation of those policies we consider to be social'. This appears to be a workable definition of policy. Policies have direct consequences for the lifelong learning sector and they are associated with education and the welfare or well-being of individuals. Alcock *et al.* (2000: 2) develop this definition of policy by arguing that UK social policy is especially concerned with five aspects of welfare: 'income maintenance and social security, health policy and services, the personal social services, education and training policy, and employment policy and housing policy'. Regarding the academic content of policy, Alcock *et al.* (2000: 2) argue that social policy is a subject that is informed by academic disciplines that include sociology, economics, politics, policy-making and history.

A number of factors have influenced UK social policy since 1834. All social policies have been influenced by historical factors. In this country, ideas about society have evolved over time. Philosophical, economic and sociological interpretations of society have developed and informed social policy. Harris (2004: 1) phrases this as being the 'ideological life' that informs the social world. It can be argued that this 'ideological life' is at the centre of many UK social policies. If social policies are introduced to help solve social problems and if they are to be evaluated as being 'effective', one can apply a cyclical process of analysis. Alcock *et al.* (2000: 3) refer to this as 'the policy cycle'. The process involves identifying a social need, proposing policy solutions, implementing these policy solutions and then evaluating their effectiveness.

Social policy is not just a study of society and its problems. It is an area of study that is intimately concerned with how to act upon and improve social problems. The social institutions that are created to ensure that social problems are resolved are also of central importance to social policy. It can be argued that a central part of the social policy process is to look at the role of the state in relation to its effectiveness in providing for its citizens.

The many complex aspects of UK society have influenced the social policies that are designed to regulate the social world. The concept of partnership and collaboration has become a key aspect of social policies in the UK. These concepts can be understood if one looks at the wider context of social policy. It can be argued that the complex heritage of New Labour and the Coalition government accounts for the focus on collaboration and partnership. It can also be claimed that all of these policy directions have fascinating implications for the lifelong learning sector.

A key factor influencing policy in the UK in recent years is the financial crisis that led to the economic recession that began in 2008. Moreover, the Coalition government in 2010 engaged immediately in what political commentators referred to as the 'bonfire of the quangos' (Selwyn, 2011). The warning signs for this new approach to technology were given when David Cameron (2009) exclaimed: 'When I see Ed Balls blow hundreds of millions on quangos like . . . BECTA, I want to say: this is my child, it's my money, give it to my head teacher instead of wasting it in Whitehall'. Weardon (2010) draws attention to the general political 'surprise' that followed the total disbandment of quangos. The association of the Coalition government with 'bland' policies was proven to be mistaken as the 'Harnessing Technology' fund witnessed a halving of its £200 million funding. This essentially represented the curtailing of new Labour's schools technology programme.

Syllabus

A syllabus is a predetermined body of knowledge that has been defined or gathered together into a discrete unit so that it might be taught to a group of students. This might, for example, be theoretical knowledge relating to Spanish literature, practical knowledge relating to brickwork or, more usually, a combination of the theoretical and the practical. In this sense, the syllabus is synonymous with the curriculum, from the point of view of content (although it is important to remember that 'curriculum' is used by education researchers and writers to explore other aspects of educational provision apart from course content).

In mainstream further education, a course syllabus might be derived from a number of different sources. Technical and vocational syllabuses, for example, need to respond to occupational standards and to the requirements of different industrial or commercial sectors (represented through the Sector Skills Councils, for example). These syllabuses change in order to respond to new innovations, new legislative requirements or other changes in economic or commercial practice. At the same time, it is important to remember that vocational courses are not simply representing the 'here and now' but are also, to varying degrees, embodying the history and tradition of a particular trade or craft. Some syllabuses will need to be rewritten on a regular basis (such as courses relating to the IT industry), whereas others will change at a slower pace (such as courses relating to wood occupations).

A syllabus from within the academic, as distinct from vocational, curriculum will respond to rather different pressures. There are no external technological or commercial drivers that significantly alter the A level English literature syllabus or the syllabus for an Access to Humanities course. Rather, the content of courses such as these is driven by broader – and arguably more difficult to define explicitly – notions of knowledge that are seen as being 'significant' or 'important'. There are several aspects to this. First, there is the sense (derived in part from the *liberal tradition* of education, which in turn looks back to classical antiquity) that there are some bodies of knowledge that people 'should' know – that are of sufficient intrinsic importance to justify their continued position within the curriculum as a whole: the benchmark of a civilised society (whatever that might mean) is that these subjects should continue to be studied. There is also a sense that the processes by which students are taught these syllabuses not only endow them with these bodies of knowledge, but also equip them more generally for life and work (although this of course refers only to very particular kinds of work). Finally, there is the concept of the transfer of learning – that studying courses that might at first glance seem to have no useful purpose is in fact an important and worthwhile process because of the more general 'critical thinking skills' or 'critical reasoning skills' that it provides.

At this point, it is important to remember that adult education provision continues to find space for courses in which the content is in some ways negotiated between the students and the tutor or the organisation offering the course (the Workers' Educational Association and the University of the Third Age are examples). In this context, the syllabus can be seen as being derived from notions of what is 'important', and from the broader preconceptions and attitudes of students and tutor.

A consideration of who is responsible for or who 'owns' a particular syllabus is therefore complex and depends on two key factors: the position of the syllabus in relation to the world of work, and the social and cultural capital attached to the syllabus.

References and further reading

Department for Education and Skills (2004) *Every Child Matters: Change for Children.* Nottingham: DfES Publications.

Giddens, A. (2004) *The Third Way and its Critics.* Cambridge: Polity Press.

James, D. and Biesta, G. (2007) *Improving Learning Cultures in Further Education.* London: Routledge.

Lumsden, E. (2005) Joined up thinking in practice: an exploration of professional collaboration, in T. Waller (ed.) *An Introduction to Early Childhood: A Multidisciplinary Approach.* London: Paul Chapman.

Rogers, C. (2004) *On Becoming a Person.* London: Constable.

Weber, M. (1983) *Max Weber on Capitalism, Bureaucracy and Religion: A Selection of Texts.* London: Allen & Unwin.

T

Teaching
Technology-enhanced learning
Theory
Training
Transformative learning

Teaching

There are a number of different approaches to teaching. There is teaching that is based upon attempting to motivate as many learners as possible. This humanist approach to teaching differs from a behaviourist concern with modifying the learning environment. Some teaching strategies attempt to make learning as active as possible for the learners. The learners are enabled to become more involved in lessons, and they are given tasks, such as problem solving. Gestalt principles for teaching are based on recommending that learners should be encouraged to discover the underlying nature of a topic or problem (in other words, the relationship between the component parts). Instruction should be based on the laws of organisation, so that there is clear planning with learners in order to organise new learning by connecting it to previous learning.

This cognitive approach to teaching is more of an academic approach based on the principle that learning occurs primarily through exposure to logically presented information. A good analogy that helps in understanding the cognitive approach to teaching is to visualise two buckets. Imagine the full bucket of the wise teacher pouring its contents into the empty bucket of the less informed learner. Cognitivism can be understood as being the 'tell' approach to teaching, so its predominant learning activity is the lecture or didactic teaching approach. Current teaching trends, however, are not always in favour of this approach to teaching and recommend shorter, 'mini-lectures' geared to a 'PlayStation', multi-media culture. The application of teacher-led pedagogy within the lifelong learning sector is important, but the amount of didactic teaching being delivered to learners needs to take into consideration the ability of the students to concentrate. Students can only be 'lectured' to for so long!

There are a number of cognitive teaching techniques used in the lifelong learning sector. These included diagrams, films, talks by subject specialists, class presentations and oral story telling. Some of the advantages of using a cognitive curriculum or approach include that the curriculum is built on a base of knowledge to extend learners' knowledge or information on concepts and rules. It can provide the platform upon which the learner can build active learning strategies. Thus it is seen as a more rapid learning method than behaviourist or humanist methods of learning.

In applying cognitive teaching techniques to the lifelong learning sector, the following guidelines need to be considered:

- information should be presented logically;
- build from an initial base of information;
- relationships between 'bits of information' are important;
- the curriculum needs to be organised to reveal its construction;
- as meaning is constructed, we need to learn a variety of different information;
- we need to develop learners as 'thinkers' if they are to become effective learners;
- we need to develop strategies and skills in learning to learn effectively;
- videos, class demonstrations, oral readings and discussions help the learning process.

In recent years, there has been a shift away from emphasising the essential importance of teaching, with an emphasis now placed upon learning. Petty (2009) describes this change in direction as a change in focus from what is being taught to what is being learnt. Urban (2008) has also drawn attention to the emphasis that is placed on the end product as opposed to the teaching process. The qualifications that are obtained by the student and the grades achieved by the teachers seem to be the most important factors influencing the lifelong learning sector. If we are in a game of representation, the focus can change accordingly. The various stakeholders in the lifelong learning sector are in turn able to influence the understanding of teaching that is then disseminated within the lifelong learning sector.

Technology-enhanced learning

Leask and Younie (2013: 280) explain technology-enhanced learning as using technology to maximise learning opportunities. An example of how technology can enhance learning in the lifelong learning sector is through the provision of an effective shared online environment. Many colleges use virtual learning environments to enhance learning through technology. The virtual learning environment (VLE) can be used to enable participants to 'move between different communities in the same environment' (Leask and Younie, 2013: 280). This approach to developing technology-based learning aims to enhance the learning process. The ideal is for a unity of 'ways of being' (pedagogy) and 'ways of knowing' (pedagogical theory and its associated policies; Urban, 2008). Carmichael and Proctor (2006) and Proctor (2007) note that there has been a development of learning that enables research-based evidence to be available online. The expectation appears to lead to a more proactive awareness of how technology-based resources can enhance learning through providing online materials as opposed to having traditional didactic teaching methods.

Sharing knowledge between practitioners, policy makers and educational researchers appears to be of vital importance if technology-enhanced learning is to occur (Barber and Mourshed, 2007). This shared knowledge may enable the development of an e-communications infrastructure that allows practitioners to develop their professional skills. Barber and Mourshed (2007) recommend the establishment of local teacher networks using technology resources. These networks ideally assume responsibility for problem solving in particular areas. If, for example, certain practitioners have a limited understanding of ICTs, the local teacher networks become responsible for addressing this technology need. Moreover, the development of what Leask and Younie (2013: 282) refer to as a national/international e-infrastructure shaped by practitioners emerges as an effective way of dealing with technology needs. For Barber and Mourshed (2007) and Leask and Younie (2013), the advantage of developing e-communication is that this in turn enhances technology-based learning.

There are criticisms of technology-enhanced learning. These critiques draw awareness to the pedagogical challenges of developing skills through applying technology (Marsh *et al.*, 2005; Plowman and Stephen, 2005; Drotner *et al.*, 2008; Yelland and Kilderry, 2010). These authors all note that ICTs can be used in a positive way to develop learning. 'E' truly can hold the potential to be 'best' if ICTs are applied in an innovative and creative way. This appears to be the way forward in applying technology to pedagogy. The challenge appears to be ensuring that technology is not used for the sake of accepting that 'e' is 'best'. Mumtaz and Hammond (2002) reveal that despite the availability of word processors in educational settings, they are still predominantly used to teach ICT skills as opposed to developing writing skills. Goldberg *et al.* (2003) also argue there can be the sort of pedagogical limitations with ICTs that Karamarski and Feldman (2000) identify in their empirical study of 'web pages'. The authors argue that although web pages may help to motivate learners, this learning strategy can be less successful than traditional ways of improving reading by using books.

Theory

A theoretical term has three components:

1. There is a logical element to a theoretical term.
2. Terms from ordinary language are adapted and in turn used to explain theories.
3. Theoretical terms are also associated with the special vocabulary and a particular use of language.

Theory is associated with many traditional forms of pedagogy. Didactic teaching and learning is linked to the dissemination of theoretical concepts. An interesting theory that has appeared within the lifelong learning sector in recent years is the theory of 'multiple forms of intelligence'. According to Gardner (2000), there are a number of different forms of intelligence. As well as linguistic and mathematical intelligences, some learners are *kinaesthetic* learners. These learners enjoy experience as opposed to theory. Gardner (2000) goes on to show that there are learners who are 'intrapersonal' and enjoy learning in isolation. In contrast, interpersonal learners learn best in a group context. There are also learners who are influenced by musical or natural criteria.

This theory contains all the elements that are listed above. The theory of multiple intelligences initially appears to have a coherence that makes it a logical theory. Terms from ordinary language are also used to explain multiple intelligences. A special language that defines multiple intelligences is in turn associated with the theory. Coffield *et al.* (2004) outline the danger of accepting the theory of multiple intelligences. These academics reveal that an acceptance of the theory of multiple intelligences has led to inspection regimes such as Ofsted advocating that teaching in the lifelong learning sector is based on an awareness of learning styles and multiple intelligences.

With respect to differing 'learning styles', Gardner argues that the 'kinaesthetic learners' who prefer learning by doing as opposed to having to rely on didactic teaching should have particular learning activities that are tailored to their learning needs. Coffield *et al.* (2004) reveal that there is no evidence that this type of learning preference actually exists. Their argument runs that the eight forms of intelligence that Gardner outlines could be increased to even more forms of intelligence. Why eight forms of intelligence? Why not nine or 11, 12, 85 or 96?

This reveals the difficulty of accepting that theories are always right. Just because a theory appears to be logical, phrased in ordinary language alongside using a special vocabulary does not mean that the theory is right. It is important to question theory. It can also be argued that the best form of teaching and learning is likely to be based on challenging theoretical concepts. Instead of accepting that there are fundamental truths within the lifelong learning sector, it is best to be flexible and innovative. Teaching is not an impossible profession. It can be argued that teaching, just like learning, is a discipline. It is important to learn from teaching experiences. Reflect on these experiences. Retain what is positive. Amend and adapt what has been less than positive. This is essentially at the centre of the craft of teaching.

Training

'Teaching and training' and 'teachers and trainers' are common expressions (and, indeed, are used within this book). For many people working in the lifelong learning sector, they are readily identifiable: 'teaching' tends to be the term used to describe instructional processes within the academic curriculum, and 'training' tends to be used more to describe the vocational curriculum, or when describing short courses of study ('training days' or 'training workshops'). 'Teaching' tends to imply the theoretical and the academic, while 'training' tends to imply the practical and the hands-on. We might see a listing for 'first-aid training' or 'teacher-training' on one page of an adult and community education prospectus, but we would not see listings for 'French language training' or 'art history training'. How can these differences be made sense of? A typical dictionary definition of 'teaching' is: 'causing a person to learn or acquire new knowledge or skill'. And at the same time, a dictionary definition of training is: 'teaching a specified skill, especially by practice'. Why should these two words cause so many problems?

The argument that we wish to present here is that there is no meaningful difference between the two activities that are known as 'teaching' and 'training' within the context of the lifelong learning sector (the use of 'training' when describing sport and exercise is somewhat different and will not be considered here). Both involve the use of a range of instructional techniques and relevant resources or materials, within theorised pedagogical contexts, by appropriately experienced and educated people. The role played by the teacher or trainer (or facilitator or instructor – the terms used are numerous and the differences between all of these are equally nebulous) is, in essence, the same. Different terms might be seen as being more naturally aligned to particular theoretical perspectives, 'trainer' to 'behaviourism', 'facilitator' to 'constructivism', and so forth, but we argue that these differences are spurious at best. Whether we define ourselves as 'trainers', as 'tutors' (which is the term more commonly used in adult and continuing education) or as 'facilitators', the reality is that these are all facets of the practice known as teaching.

The use of the term 'training' is based in part, therefore, on the adoption of a particular theoretical or philosophical perspective relating to learning. It is also based in part on the continuing (despite various efforts to the contrary) division between the academic curriculum and the vocational curriculum. Historically, the academic curriculum has enjoyed a privileged position in relation to the vocational curriculum in the UK (in contrast to continental Europe). Further education colleges continue to be underfunded compared with sixth-form colleges, and teachers in further education continue to have a more precarious professional status than those in schools (the recent decision to return teacher education for the lifelong learning sector to a voluntary status notwithstanding). School teaching has long been a 'graduate profession' (whatever that might mean), in contrast to teaching in colleges or in adult education settings. From this perspective, the use of the terms 'teacher' and 'trainer' can be seen as part of the academic/vocational and graduate/non-graduate divide. 'Teachers' are graduates who work within the academic curriculum; 'trainers' are (predominantly) non-graduates who work within the vocational curriculum. And by extension, 'teaching' occupies a superior social and political position than 'training'. This is a conceptualisation that we reject. At the same time, it remains the case that practitioners may choose to identify themselves as 'teachers' or 'trainers', alongside other terms such as 'tutors', 'facilitators' and so forth. This is entirely understandable, but the differing levels of social and political capital that these terms enjoy should be seen as troublesome and remain an issue for critical reflection.

Transformative learning

The concept of transformative learning is most closely associated with the work of Jack Mezirow (1927–), Emeritus Professor of Adult and Continuing Education at Columbia University in the USA. The theoretical roots of Mezirow's work can be seen in the earlier work of Paulo Freire (1921–1997), educator and author of, among other works, *Pedagogy of the Oppressed* (1972) and Jürgen Habermas (1929–), a sociologist and philosopher. The empirical roots of Mezirow's concept of transformative learning can be seen in his early research of women returning to education and the workplace (Mezirow, 1991). Mezirow himself defines transformative learning as 'the process by which we transform problematic frames of reference (mindsets, habits of mind, meaning perspectives) – sets of assumption and expectation – to make them more inclusive, discriminating, open, reflective and emotionally able to change' (Mezirow, 2006: 26).

The central idea behind transformative learning is a focus not on the acquisition of bodies of skills or knowledge (which Mezirow argues are important, but should not be seen as the 'end goal' of an educative process), but on the processes that lead the learner to experience a shift or transformation in perspective or understanding relating to the rules or structures of the world around us, through the related processes of (1) critical reflection and

(2) participation in discourse with others. In this way, the adult learner is able to move beyond what Mezirow, drawing on the work of Habermas, describes as 'instrumental' learning and 'communicative' learning. Instrumental learning involves the kinds of activity that allow people to learn how to do things – how to repair bicycles, how to test someone's eyesight or how to solve quadratic equations. It is about *knowing*. Communicative learning is the kind of learning that happens through the process of communicating with other people – through speech or through writing. It is about *making judgements*. Both of these kinds of learning are necessary and important, according to Mezirow, but they need to be complemented by a third kind of learning – *transformative learning* – which is the kind of learning that allows the learner to begin to understand, critique, and then act to make a difference to the society (and by extension, the world) around them. This is the element of Mezirow's work that reflects the influence of Freire, specifically Freire's concept of critical pedagogy – a pedagogy designed to empower learning in a political sense.

It is important to note that transformative learning is not a phenomenon that excludes either instrumental or communicative learning (it is also important to note that 'instrumental', as used by Habermas and Mezirow, has a rather different meaning to 'instrumental' as used when describing audit and performativity cultures). Rather, a process of transformative learning can be facilitated as a consequence of instrumental or communicative learning. Or, to put it another way, a process of emancipatory learning, of shift in perspective leading to a new and critical understanding of the social, political and/or cultural context in which the learner finds her or himself, can be begun through any other programme of learning, whether it is a course for car mechanics or an English literature course. For practitioners in adult education, therefore, Mezirow's concept of transformative learning is understandably compelling. Many practitioners in adult education retain a political and philosophical commitment to their pedagogic practice that can be lost sight of in the instrumental and target-driven environment of the further education college. But it is important to remember that Mezirow's concept rests not solely on an approach to pedagogy that foregrounds an open, 'democratic' classroom, but on a wider philosophy of the purpose of adult education in society, which is to scrutinise that society and find ways of effecting change.

References and further reading

Audi, R. (1995) *The Cambridge Dictionary of Philosophy*. Cambridge: Cambridge University Press.

Barber, M. and Moursed, M. (2007) *How the world's best-performing school systems come out on top* [online]. London: McKinsey & Co. Available from: http://mckinseyonsociety.com/downloads/reports/Education/Worlds_School_Systems_Final.pdf [accessed 1 September 2012].

Carmichael, P. and Procter, R. (2006) *IT for Education Research: Using New Technology to Enhance a Complex Research Programme*. Teaching and Learning Research Briefing No. 16. London: University of London Institute of Education.

Coffield, F., Moseley, D., Hall, E. and Ecclestone, K. (2004) *Should We be Using Learning Styles? What Research has to Say to Practice*. London: Learning and Skills Research Centre.

Drotner, K., Siggard Jensen, H. and Christian Schroeder, K. (2008) *Informal Learning and Digital Media*. Newcastle: Cambridge Scholars Publishing.

Freire, P. (1972) *Pedagogy of the Oppressed*. Harmondsworth: Penguin.

Gardner, H. (2000) *Intelligence Reframed: Multiple Intelligences for the 21st Century*. New York: Basic Books.

Goldberg, A., Russell, M. and Cook, A. (2003) The effects of computers on students' writing: a meta-analysis from 1992–2002, *Journal of Technology, Learning and Assessment*, 2(1), 1–52.

Karamarski, B. and Feldman, Y. (2000) Internet in the classroom: effects on reading, comprehension and metacognition, *Educational Media International*, 37(3), 149–55.

Leask, M. and Younie, S. (2013) National models for continuing professional development: the challenges of twenty-first century knowledge management, *Professional Development in Education*, 39(2), 273–87.

Marsh, J., Brooks, G., Hughes, J., Ritchie, L., Roberts, S. and Wright, K. (2005) *Digital Beginnings: Young People's Use of Popular Culture, New Media and New Technologies*. Sheffield: University of Sheffield.

Mezirow, J. (1991) *Transformative Dimensions of Adult Learning*. San Francisco, CA: Jossey-Bass.

Mezirow, J. (2006) An overview on transformative learning, in P. Sutherland and J. Crowther (eds.) *Lifelong Learning: Concepts and Contexts*. London: Routledge.

Mumtaz, S. and Hammond, M. (2002) The word processor re-visited: observations on the use of the word processor to develop children's literacy at Key Stage 2, *British Journal of Educational Technology*, 33(3), 345–7.

Petty, G. (2009) *Teaching Today* (4th edn.). Cheltenham: Nelson Thornes.

Plowman, L. and Stephen, C. (2005) Children, play and computers in pre-school education, *British Journal of Educational Technology*, 36(2), 145–57.

Procter, R. (2007) Collaboration, coherence and capacity-building: the role of DSpace in supporting and understanding the TLRP, *Technology, Pedagogy and Education*, 16, 269–88.

Urban, M. (2008) Dealing with uncertainty: challenges and possibilities for the early childhood profession, *European Early Childhood Education Research Journal*, 16(2), 135–52.

Yelland, N. and Kilderry, A. (2010) Becoming numerate with information technologies in the twenty-first century, *International Journal of Early Years Education*, 18(2), 91–106.

U

Underachievement

Underachievement in the lifelong learning sector is associated with students not acquiring the grades that they 'should'. All sorts of target are set for educational achievement. These targets come from the government via the Department for Education DfE). The DfE has a series of performance tables that outline which educational establishments have learners who are achieving and underachieving. We need to consider the complex range of factors responsible for underachievement, which include the social background of the learners. Bourdieu (1993) would argue that a main factor influencing the achievement of learners is their 'cultural capital' (or their ability to cope with formal education). Particular children from disadvantaged backgrounds do not appear to have the cultural capital that is required to achieve well in educational settings. Other factors that appear to influence achievement include teaching, learning, intelligence, application and motivation. This complex range of factors has an influence on whether a learner achieves or underachieves.

Underachievement is associated with controversy. The primary focus of Ofsted appears to be the teaching and learning that occurs within the classroom. Less attention is paid to the learner's social background. The focus is placed upon what is happening within the classroom environment. Another controversial feature of Ofsted's interpretation of underachievement is that social deprivation is not taken into consideration as much as it should be, something that is revealed by national tables of achievement. The area of the country that the school is in and its levels (or otherwise) of social deprivation are not given the same attention that is devoted to the learning and teaching that takes place in the classroom.

Moreover, learners within the lifelong learning sector are often characterised by particular needs. A reason why these learners are in the lifelong learning sector as opposed to being in school is because they have struggled within a school environment. This factor does not appear to be regarded extensively by Ofsted. The pressure to achieve high pass rates appears to be the dominant concern. For Minott (2010), the crucial element for developing teaching and learning is 'reflection'. Minott (2010: 327) argues that reflecting on an 'understanding of what works' within teaching and learning informs the effective teaching that enhances student learning. It can be argued that this process is more likely to occur within the lifelong learning sector when the variety of factors influencing achievement is taken into consideration. This holds the potential for the development of a new pedagogy that is not based on meeting standards but, conversely, encourages teachers and learners to develop the curriculum for academic reasons alone.

Urban (2008, 2009) uses the film 'The Wizard of Oz' as an analogy for what appears to be happening within the UK education system. Just as the characters in the film appear to focus on their final destination, so the UK education system seems to be obsessed with final achievement (or underachievement). Urban makes the point that if this is the case, the educational processes that are happening within the educational institutions are missed. The priority appears to be the qualifications as opposed to the processes that lead to those qualifications.

References and further reading

Bourdieu, P. (1993) *Outline of a Theory of Practice*. Cambridge: Cambridge University Press.

Minott, M.A. (2010) Reflective teaching as self-directed professional development: building practical or work-related knowledge, *Professional Development in Education*, 36(1), 325–38.

Urban, M. (2008) Dealing with uncertainty: challenges and possibilities for the early childhood profession, *European Early Childhood Education Research Journal*, 16(2), 135–52.

Urban, M. (2009) *Strategies for change: rethinking professional development to meet the challenges of diversity in the early years profession*. Paper presented at the International Professional Development Association Conference, 27–28 November, Birmingham.

V

Values
Vocational education
Vocationalism and new vocationalism
Voice

Values

Values are related to the priorities that are given to the lifelong learning sector. Different groups of individuals appear to value aspects of the lifelong learning sector in different ways. Teachers may place an emphasis on the importance of the value of pedagogy. Learners may place an emphasis on the value of completing their programme assignments successfully. Managers may place a value on managing the resources within the lifelong learning sector in an efficient way. All of these different values shape our understanding of the lifelong learning sector. Moreover, what is valued appears to change over time and space. The existing educational *Zeitgeist* is likely to influence the values of the lifelong learning sector.

Changing values within education links to the work of Michel Foucault (1977) and his examination of the changing nature of power relations within social space. Foucault (1986: 99) has commented on the changing nature of power within Western societies. Power is not understood in isolation from time and space. Conversely, expressions of power depend on time and space. There is no statement in general, no free neutral, independent statement; but a statement always belongs to a series or a whole, always plays a role among other statements, deriving support from and distinguishing itself from them: it is always part of a network of statements, in which it has a role, however minimal, to play.

The argument runs that in societies such as that in the UK there has been a move away from 'public executions' to more complex manifestations of power in the form of 'observation' and 'surveillance'. Foucault's ideas may help to explain the changing values that are expressed within the lifelong learning sector. This reflects the move away from traditional, 'teacher-centred' models of learning to newer pedagogical themes with an emphasis on 'learning'. These models of pedagogy appear to have been influenced by changing regimes of social power. This means that those teachers who base their teaching on traditional models of pedagogy are unable to relate to the discourse of newer models of teaching and learning.

Tedder and Lawy (2009) have identified that the differing values of different stakeholders in the lifelong learning sector influences their perception of learning and teaching. The trainees, managers, and tutors in their research sample had differing interpretations of the purpose of mentoring. Tedder and Lawy (2009: 417) outline that the trainees, tutors and managers appeared to be more interested in the developmental nature of mentoring as opposed to interpreting the process in a judgemental way. It can be argued that this is because mentoring is not accepted as a sound part of the educational context because it is not currently understood as constituting accepted educational cultural capital. To paraphrase Bourdieu, it is viewed more like an ill-fitting product in the current educational market. There are many other examples of educational phenomena in the lifelong learning sector such as this. The interpretation of the curriculum and the purpose of the lifelong learning sector depend upon the values of the stakeholders. One of the reasons why the lifelong learning sector is such a fascinating area of study is because of this variation of values.

Vocational education

Vocational education is associated with education that results in employability. There are differing interpretations of education that are held by various educationalists. Not all of these educationalists would be in favour of vocational education.

Coffield *et al.* (2004), Hale (2008), Lieberman (2009), Lucas (2007), Urban (2008) and Wenger (1998) draw attention to the variability of interpretation that is present within educational contexts in general. The Latin verb *educere* (with its implication that individuals and groups can be enabled to see the world differently) can be used to acknowledge the role that education can have in helping to realise creative potential. The interest in this understanding of education is associated with the emergence of the concept of reflective practice as opposed to emphasising the importance of vocational education. The 'new pedagogy' that Tummons (2011a: 481) refers to as 'a low stakes rather than a high stakes paradigm' encourages academics and learners to develop the curriculum for academic reasons alone.

The potential tension between vocational education and other interpretations of the role of education reveals that there are differing discursive interpretations of educational contexts. Michel Foucault (1977) regards discourse as being formative. Foucault is concerned with what is occurring within institutions and the way that power is being exercised in his account of how discourse influences social contexts like education (Hudson, 2003: 134). Foucault is essentially providing a micro rather than a macro analysis by providing a dystopian account of post-Enlightenment events within which there occurs a Nietzschean will to power, oppression, disciplinary regulation and subjugation. McNay (1994: 5) argues that a central concern of Foucault is the way the individual is formed as a by-product of discursive formations linked to the politics of power and the demand for social order.

Foucault's (1977) work develops the argument that 'discourse' or 'conversations' within society in general and within particular aspects of society such as education are linked to changes in power regimes. This argument is made in the following reflection:

> The judges of normality are present everywhere. We are in the society of the teacher-judge, the doctor-judge, the educator-judge, the social worker-judge; it is on them that the universal reign of the normative is based and each individual wherever he may find himself, subjects it to his body.
>
> (Foucault, 1977: 304)

Foucault is arguing that power relationships depend upon current interpretations of social space. This suggests that the conversations that academics and learners have about education are a reflection of changing power dynamics within social space.

This accounts for why we have changing interpretations of the purpose of education. The influence of political and economic ideas in education in the UK accounts for why vocational education is such an important component of the lifelong learning sector. The current Coalition government and New Labour have both intervened in shaping the priorities of the lifelong learning sector. This is why vocational education (or education that helps with employability) is so important. Foucault's (1977) work outlines that developments such as this are a product of discourse. The way that the educational context is understood and talked about becomes the determining factor with respect to what is valued and held to be important. Whether or not vocational education continues to be a vital component of the lifelong learning sector remains to be seen. If new interpretations of education appear, which place an emphasis on individual creativity instead of employability, we may see a new interpretation of the purpose of the lifelong learning sector. Coffield (2006) in particular has drawn attention to the concerns that many educationalists have about the influence that politicians and economists can have over educational contexts. The concern is based on the implications of decisions about education being made because of political and economic agendas.

Vocationalism and new vocationalism

When used in the context of curriculum, the term 'vocational' refers in the very broadest terms to education and training provision that pertains to vocational occupations, as delivered in further education colleges and, increasingly, in schools and adult education centres too. Typical examples include motor vehicle, hairdressing and plumbing courses. Vocationalism is the political and cultural emphasis that has, historically, been placed on vocational education and training and, specifically, on the need to ensure that sufficient people receive an education that is appropriately linked to the world of work, and that has been designed in such a way that the perceived needs of employers have ben accounted for.

The apogee of vocationalism can be seen through studying the so-called 'Great Debate' – the speech given by James Callaghan, the then Prime Minister, at Ruskin College Oxford in 1976 (Tummons, 2011b). To his supporters, Callaghan's speech was a timely critique of a curriculum that failed adequately to prepare people for industry and commerce:

> I am concerned on my journeys to find complaints from industry that new recruits from the schools sometimes do not have the basic tools to do the job that is required […] I have been concerned to find out that many of our best trained students who have completed the higher levels of education at university or polytechnic have no desire to join industry […] There seems to be a need for more technological bias in science teaching that will lead towards practical applications in industry rather than towards academic studies.
>
> (Callaghan, 1976)

At the heart of this vocationalism lay a particular model of employment that – put simply – saw further education colleges working relatively independently from one another, responding to local and regional employment and labour market pressures, where young people who attended college, undertook apprentices or participated in day-release training programmes were trained for roles in specific industries and trades (Parry, 1989).

The decline and (arguably) political neglect of much of England's traditional manufacturing sector in the 1970s and 1980s rendered this model of vocationalism redundant, leading to the emergence of a new vocationalism. Instead of providing a vocational education for people who would be working in particular industrial or manufacturing sectors, colleges instead had to respond to two new pressures. The first of these pressures was the need to provide a more 'general' vocational education to students following more ambiguous pathways into employment. In this model, students would be equipped with 'transferable', general skills that would prepare them for the workplace, rather than sector-specific or subject-based skills (Turner, 2007). The second pressure was the need to keep more people in education and training for longer in order to ease pressure on a labour market that was already struggling to cope with the number of people seeking to enter. Successive measures enacted by governments of all hues to increase participation rates and ages (rendering the term 'post-compulsory' education and training redundant when considering students aged 16–19) required the expansion of the vocational curriculum to include both new courses that reflected the expanding service sectors and new curricula that would be sufficiently attractive to sustain the engagement of more and more young people who were now being required, and variously pressurised or induced, to remain in education and training for longer, irrespective of the extent to which they were aligned to the world of work.

Voice

The need to listen and respond to the student voice is not a new phenomenon, but has in recent years gained in prominence. Arguably, the wider history of liberal adult education in the UK cannot be understood without recognising the role played by the student body in shaping or negotiating the curriculum that was offered by organisations such as the Workers' Educational Association (WEA), or by university-based extra-mural departments of continuing education, which would frequently offer courses and even recruit specific people to teach them in response to requests from the students. While the provision of negotiated curricula such as these is now much less common (although the WEA and the University of the Third Age do continue to offer some curricula in this fashion and, moreover, rely on the student body for a significant amount of their administration), the increasing prominence given to the student voice (across all educational sectors, not just in lifelong learning) needs to be understood as being the product of a number of social and political shifts.

The first factor leading to a greater prominence for the student voice can be found in the rise of accountability and *audit* cultures and concurrent shifts in definitions of *professionalism*. As the work of professional groups – including teachers – has come under greater scrutiny, the idea that the professional 'always knows best' has been superseded by the idea that the users of a service – in this instance, students at a further education college or adult education centre – should be meaningfully involved or consulted in relation to the service that is being offered. Obtaining evaluative feedback from service users has become an increasingly common feature of different audit and inspection processes. Thus, one of the parameters of an Ofsted inspection is the extent to which student feedback is obtained and then acted upon. Similarly, internal or external verification events at further education colleges often include a 'student panel' or similar, when students on the programme being audited can provide feedback to the auditor. The extent to which such events can be seen as being authentic is questionable. They are invariably held during the working day: full-time students (many of whom also work and/or have family responsibilities) find attending such events difficult – part-time students, more so. It is not uncommon for students to be 'hand-picked' for events such as these.

Related to this is the broader concept of the student as stakeholder, in turn derived from stakeholder theory. According to stakeholder theory, which originates from business and organisational studies, a stakeholder is anyone who has a legitimate interest in the conduct, welfare, organisation, and practice of any institution that they are involved with – as a user, an employee, a sub-contractor, and so on. As so-called 'business facing' models have been applied to education over the last 20 years or so, so has the concept of 'stakeholder' been taken up and applied to all of those who are deemed to be involved in education. Students, funding agencies, inspectors, parents and employers are all examples of stakeholders in the lifelong learning sector, whose responses to and evaluations of the service that they receive are carefully recorded in inspection reports, parents' evenings, the minutes of user group meetings, and so forth. Finally, it should be noted that stakeholder models are rather different from models of education and training that position the student as a consumer of an educational 'product', which, it is argued, distort the relationship between students and teachers through the erroneous use of notions such as 'value for money' and 'consumer rights'. At the same time, it is important to note the criticism that surrounds the concept of student voice. Asking for student representatives to speak at a college governors' meeting is appropriate; asking them to evaluate the pedagogic strategies that they are exposed to is not.

References and further reading

Callaghan, J. (1976) *A rational debate based on the facts*. Speech delivered at Ruskin College Oxford, 18 October.

Coffield, F. (2006) *Running ever faster down the wrong road*. Inaugural Lecture, University of London Institute of Education, London.

Coffield, F., Moseley, D., Hall, E. and Ecclestone, K. (2004) *Learning Styles and Pedagogy in Post-16 Learning: A Systematic and Critical Review*. London: LSDA.

Foucault, M. (1977) *Discipline and Punish*. London: Allen Lane.

Foucault, M. (1986) *The Archaeology of Knowledge*. London: Tavistock.

Hale, J.A. (2008) *A Guide to Curriculum Planning*. Thousand Oaks, CA: Corwin Press.

Hudson, B. (2003) *Understanding Justice: An Introduction to Ideas, Perspectives and Controversies in Modern Penal History*. Buckingham: Open University Press.

Lieberman, J. (2009) Reinventing teacher professional norms and identities: the role of lesson study and learning communities, *Professional Development in Education*, 35(1), 83–99.

Lucas, N. (2007) The in-service training of adult literacy, numeracy and English for Speakers of Other Languages teachers in England; the challenges of a 'standards-led model', *Journal of In-Service Education*, 33(1), 125–42.

McNay, L. (1994) *Foucault: A Critical Introduction*. Cambridge: Polity Press.

Parry, G. (1989) The 'new vocationalism': further education and local labour markets, *Journal of Education Policy*, 4(3), 227–44.

Tedder, M. and Lawy, R. (2009) The pursuit of 'excellence': mentoring in further education initial teacher training in England, *Journal of Vocational Education and Training*, 61(4), 413–29.

Tummons, J. (2011a) It sort of feels uncomfortable: problematising the assessment of reflective practice, *Studies in Higher Education*, 36(4), 471–83.

Tummons, J. (2011b) *Curriculum Studies in the Lifelong Learning Sector* (2nd edn.). London: Sage/Learning Matters.

Turner, A. (2007) Key skills or key subjects?, in D. Hayes, T. Marshall and A. Turner (eds.) *A Lecturer's Guide to Further Education*. Maidenhead: McGraw-Hill.

Urban, M. (2008) Dealing with uncertainty: challenges and possibilities for the early childhood profession, *European Early Childhood Education Research Journal*, 16(2), 135–52.

Wenger, E. (1998) *Communities of Practice: Learning, Meaning and Identity*. New York: Cambridge University Press.

W

Widening participation
Wolf report
Work-based learning
Workers' Educational Association

Widening participation

Widening participation refers to the agenda of recent UK governments that attempts to include as many students as possible within formal education. The last New Labour government made the claim that it wanted to see 50 per cent of the population attending higher education. To realise this ambition, it is necessary for as many learners as possible to be included within the formal curriculum. The consequences for the curriculum within the lifelong learning sector are significant. As opposed to expecting learners to adapt to the curriculum, the recommendation from the politicians has been to adapt the curriculum to accommodate as many learners as possible. This has significant implications for the curriculum.

The traditional curriculum within the UK is academic and based upon an assessment of intellectual ability. A 'sink or swim' mentality occurred within educational processes. The students who were able to pass the '11 plus' entrance examination (or pay for elite education) received a formal education. Those unable to qualify for this education completed technical education and left school with no formal qualifications. By the end of the 1950s, the deficiencies of this education system (based on the concern that a majority received little formal education) resulted in the emergence of the comprehensive education system. With the abolition of (most) grammar schools and technical schools, it was almost the end of the two-tier education system.

In a further development of the UK education system, we began to see the emergence of a widening participation agenda following the creation of the post-1992 universities in the UK (the former polytechnics). The realisation that large numbers of students are included within higher education has led to the development of the widening participation agenda. As opposed to assuming that students can cope with academic work, all sorts of support networks have been established to help these students. These include learning support tutors who are present to help students to complete their academic work. The emphasis is placed on 'learning and teaching' as opposed to 'teaching and learning' in order to enable the curriculum to be made accessible to as many learners as possible. As opposed to having summative assessments based on formal examinations, coursework is used to assess the students.

The English university system has moved away from an elite, publicly funded system paying the fees of a minority of students. Whereas only 5 per cent of the school leaving population went to university in the 1960s, university education has been transformed to currently include 45 per cent of school leavers (Brennan *et al.*, 2009). As well as this demographic change within English universities, there has been an evolution of the academic curriculum of UK universities. The traditional professions of medicine, the law and education – with their associated academic degrees – have been joined by vocational professions, including nursing and social work. There is, however, the perception that 'quality' degrees are associated with particular universities and specific academic programmes. Critics of the widening participation agenda claim that education has become 'dumbed down' in a concern over academic standards. The basis of this critique is that intellectual abilities are finite. The argument runs that the inclusion of more than 40 per cent of the population in the university process must lead to a drop in standards at universities due to the finite nature of intellectual capabilities.

Wolf report

The Review of Vocational Education conducted by Professor Alison Wolf of King's College London, and hence known as the Wolf Report (2011), was commissioned by Michael Gove, Secretary of State for Education, in 2010, and published in the following year. The Wolf Report provides a comprehensive and arresting account of the current and recent state of 14–19 vocational education provision, perhaps best summarised by the central message that the vocational education system contains many examples of excellent practice (the examples given in the report include companies such as Rolls-Royce and Airbus, and further education colleges such as Macclesfield and Westminster Kingsway) that work in spite of, rather than because of, the structures that underpin the vocational education system as a whole, which is described in the report as being wildly variable in quality.

Wolf's report is appropriately situated within and mindful of a political and historical milieu of changing employment patterns, the decline of traditional manufacturing, and the growth of more transient and temporary forms of employment. Within this context, she argues that the current vocational education system is in several key ways failing the students that it purports to serve:

- Too many young people continue to fail to achieve good grades in English and mathematics at GCSE – positioned as essential key skills for all students aged 14–19, irrespective of whether they follow the 'vocational curriculum' or the 'academic curriculum'.
- The vocational education system is rigid and unresponsive [Wolf uses the term 'sclerotic' (Wolf, 2011: 21)], expensive, and overly centralised (the last being a particularly interesting point bearing in mind the fact that this report was published almost 20 years after incorporation – one reading of this might be that incorporation has failed in two of its avowed aims – of rendering further education colleges more responsive to local pressures, and of making them more competitive in financial terms).
- Too many awarding bodies are offering too many qualifications. Moreover, the real-world value of too many qualifications is inflated. This can be seen in terms of equivalences (the ways in which a certain number of vocational qualifications are deemed to be 'worth' a particular number of GCSEs according to a predetermined tariff). It can also be seen in the proliferation of vocational qualifications at Levels 1 and 2 (which are delivered in both schools and in further education colleges) that fail to help young people gain meaningful employment and also fail to help them progress to higher education.

The recommendations made by the report included reducing the number of vocational qualifications, requiring all school/college leavers to obtain maths and English GSCEs (or equivalent), and changing the tariff attached to qualifications so that institutions will not be encouraged to enter students for qualifications that will not lead to progression (to either employment or higher education). Other recommendations included improvements to work experience (for full-time students, not for apprentices), and allowing further education teachers with QTLS (Qualified Teacher, Learning and Skills) to teach in schools (thereby creating professional parity with schoolteachers with QTS – Qualified Teacher Status).

The Wolf Report, therefore, consists of a powerful critique of vocational education, although it is important to stress that some of the issues raised had already been identified by other researchers and writers (Atkins, 2009). The Coalition government, in its formal response, accepted all of the recommendations made in the Wolf Report. At the time of writing, it is unclear whether further changes to a sector of education that has already seen many changes in curriculum, funding, and organisation during the last two decades (Edward *et al.*, 2007) will have any meaningful impact.

Work-based learning

One of the arguments presented in this book is that learning happens all of the time, irrespective of whether the context of that learning is *formal* or *informal*. Indeed, a *social* theory of learning proposes that learning is happening 'all of the time', and the value or worth of that learning is dictated by the context in which it happens rather than the nature of the learning itself. From this perspective, it is clear that much learning takes place at work (here defined in terms of paid employment or voluntary work, or work experience gained during a placement in a recognised institutional setting). We define work-based learning, therefore, as learning that takes place at and through work, in either a formal or informal context. The formal provision of work-based learning is commonly linked to wider notions of employability and might relate either to specific occupational skills or competencies, or to *generic* or transferable skills that are perceived as being desirable for employees to possess or develop further. Formal provision of work-based learning such as this is typically organised around a recognised curriculum, accompanied by relevant public assessment systems. National Vocational Qualifications (NVQs) are the most obvious example of work-based qualifications. Informal work-based learning, by contrast, is simply a term used by writers and researchers to describe the incidental learning that takes place in the workplace but which is not formally recognised or captured within a qualifications framework. Work-based learning constitutes a key feature of more than just NVQ provision, however. Apprenticeships rest on notions of work-based learning, as do college and university courses that require students to undertake work placements as part of the curriculum (childcare courses being one example). Other courses within the further education curriculum also require students to be in some form of paid employment in order to be able to access the course.

Within formal contexts such as those outlined above, work-based learning is positioned as a necessary element of a formal curriculum that runs alongside and complements the learning that (in some cases) will take place in the workshop or classroom. In this sense, it is the authenticity of the workplace that gives value to this learning: work-based learning is required to be based in the real world of work, not in a simulated environment. Those curricula that aim to prepare students for the world of work but which do not contain a formal requirement for a placement, for day or block release or other similar access to the workplace are referred to instead as work related. Work-*related* learning courses are equally common in the further education sector in particular and often follow the same syllabuses as work-based learning programmes, but they do not provide certification of occupational competence: they do not certify the student as being 'work ready'.

To provide meaningful work experience for students, many further education colleges have established business-style environments within their institutions. Common examples include hair and beauty salons, restaurants and travel agencies, which are normally open to the public. While these environments are undoubtedly of value, the kinds of learning that they offer are subject to some debate. The extent to which the kinds of learning that students participate in while working in college-based training salons, for example, have been shown to be quite distinct from the learning that accrues from working in a professional salon as an apprentice or on day release (Billett, 2008). The best efforts of colleges to create authentic working environments notwithstanding, college-based salons or training restaurants are self-evidently qualitatively different to their 'real-world' counterparts. As such, the extent to which such institutions offer work-based or work-related learning continues to be argued over.

Workers' Educational Association

Albert Mansbridge and Frances Jane Pringle (who were married) founded the Workers' Educational Association (WEA) in 1903, although for the first two years of its existence it was known as 'the association to promote the higher education of working men'. Mansbridge had left school aged 14 and had attended university extension classes, the provision of which was increasing in the late nineteenth century. These extension classes were very much tailored to a middle- and upper-class student body, and Mansbridge and Pringle were concerned to extend such provision to the working class. The WEA grew rapidly – from 1905, Mansbridge worked for the WEA on a full-time basis – and quickly began to establish links with universities, particularly during the period after 1945 when extra-mural university departments experienced rapid growth. Over the last 30 or so years, the 'liberal tradition' of adult education has declined in the face of vocationalism, on the one hand, and mass higher education, on the other, and university departments of adult and continuing education have receded (Taylor, 1996). But the WEA has in recent times managed to shift in response to wider political change, while at the same time continuing to offer a considerable range of curricula to diverse student populations ranging from people with mental health difficulties to adult learners who need to develop literacy and numeracy skills, to people who use adult education classes as a way of sustaining a hobby.

Beyond its national headquarters, the WEA is arranged on a regional basis in the UK – all professionally staffed. Each region consists of a number of different local branches, organised by volunteers who engage in activities that range from organising venues for classes to interviewing the part-time tutors who make up the vast majority of the teaching workforce. A considerable number of people are involved. At the time of writing, there are over 400 local branches, run by approximately 3000 volunteers. Approximately 2000 part-time tutors work for the WEA, some teaching just one or two courses, others teaching a number of courses across more than one branch. Over 70,000 people attend over 9000 different WEA courses each year.

It is perhaps unsurprising that the work of the WEA has changed considerably over time. The majority of students on WEA courses are now female and new areas of provision (such as English for speakers of other languages and community education) are relatively recent arrivals. By contrast, courses in the liberal arts and humanities have for decades been a mainstay of WEA provision. As with over providers, changes in policy and in funding structures have also influenced curriculum provision: the changes to local education authority practice that saw further education colleges removed from LEA control in the early 1990s also saw wider changes to the funding of adult and community education. Local government provision declined and WEA provision found itself subject to the same kinds of audit and evaluation as schools and colleges. Ways had to be found of formally assessing student learning (a point of considerable theoretical and philosophical disagreement among adult educators) that would not generate barriers to participation. At the same time, WEA provision fell under the inspection regimes of the Adult Learning Inspectorate, which was subsequently absorbed into Ofsted in 2007.

Mansbridge himself was an advocate of what might be termed 'education for education's sake': he saw adult education as being about individual self-development, and saw the WEA as a vehicle for allowing the mass of the working population to have access to the 'high arts and culture' that had historically been the preserve of the universities, unrelated to the social and political context (Taylor, 1996). While the WEA's contemporary turn towards 'employability' and 'community' courses might seem far removed from Mansbridge's ethos, it can also be seen as a necessary and important shift if the needs of an increasingly diverse adult education population are to be met in such a way that the overriding ethos of the WEA – of providing a second chance for learning – is to be maintained both now and in the future.

References and further reading

Atkins, L. (2009) *Invisible Students, Impossible Dreams: Experiencing Vocational Education 14–19*. Stoke on Trent: Trentham Books.

Billett, S. (2008) Learning through work: exploring instances of relational interdependencies, *International Journal of Educational Research*, 47(4), 232–40.

Brennan, J., Edmunds, R., Houston, M., Jary, D., Lebeau, Y., Osborne, M. and Richardson, J.T.E. (2009) *Improving What is Learned at University: An Exploration of the Social and Organisational Diversity of University Education*. London: Routledge.

Edward, S., Coffield, F., Steer, R. and Gregson M. (2007) Endless change in the learning and skills sector: the impact on teaching staff, *Journal of Vocational Education and Training*, 57(2), 155–73.

Fieldhouse, R. (1996) The Workers' Educational Association, in R. Fieldhouse (ed.) *A History of Modern British Adult Education*. Leicester: NIACE.

Taylor, R. (1996) Preserving the liberal tradition in new times, in J. Wallis (ed.) *Liberal Adult Education: The End of an Era?* Nottingham: University of Nottingham.

Wolf, A. (2011) *Review of Vocational Education* (The Wolf Report). London: Department for Education/Department for Business, Innovation and Skills.

Y

> Youth work

Youth work

Youth work refers to work that is done with young people. Whereas 'early years' refers to those who are aged from birth to 8 years, youth work is often associated with the ages of 9–19 years. A number of therapies (or ways of working) are associated with youth work. These therapies attempt to help young people to develop physically, intellectually, emotionally, and socially. One of the most important ways of working with young people is based on the humanist philosophy of Carl Rogers.

The humanist philosophy of Carl Rogers is at the centre of what is deemed as being 'good practice' within youth work. Rogers proposes an egalitarian model of practice in which the practitioner is not aloof from the client but 'with' the client. Empathy is a particularly important aspect of the Rogerian way. The practitioner must be there for the young person and be prepared to be genuine and assertive. According to Rogers, a genuine practitioner can enable a young person's growth and development.

Effective practice is facilitated upon resolving the 'would/should dilemma'. Rogers considers that this dilemma is the cause of anxiety, which, in turn, prevents development. Practitioners should also direct their clients towards their 'beautiful inner self'. Rogers believes that all individuals are innately good and that it is only the tension that results from a 'would/should dilemma' that makes the individual a less than good person. Through a genuine and empathetic relationship, it is postulated that the 'would/should dilemma' will be replaced by an assertive awareness of one's inner goodness. Although there are many applications for this type of therapy, the generalising assumptions that are made within humanism can result in difficulties.

There appear to be limitations in the application of Rogerian client-centred therapy. For clients to accept the importance of resolving the 'would/should dilemma', it is important that they share similar values to the therapist. The client needs to accept that the values of the therapist are important so that there can be a link between what both therapist and client want to achieve. There are, however, many instances when the values of the young person may be opposed to the values of the therapist. This can be exemplified within a life-long learning environment in which the learners do not want to achieve what their teachers perceive to be important. This is supported by research on the so-called 'chavs' subculture within the North-East of England. Anne Watson (2004) also acknowledges this in her discussion of the failings of the wider academic curriculum within the UK. Watson argues that it is not so much that the curriculum is a 'bad idea', but that there is little awareness of how to unite the values of the young people and their teachers. Thus Rogerian client-centred therapy will not work because there is no common understanding of what is important and achievable. It is all very well to say that a 'would/should dilemma' should be resolved but a young person can only be directed to their 'inner beautiful self' if they perceive that self through a shared sense of identity with their therapist. Malim and Birch (1998: 803) develop this criticism by arguing that a critical limitation with humanist therapies relates to the assumption that 'self-actualisation' is a principal human motivation. Self-actualisation may motivate particular groups of individuals but it cannot be assumed to be a universal characteristic of every human being at every point in time.

References and further reading

Malim, T. and Birch, A. (1998) *Introductory Psychology*. London: Palgrave Macmillan.

Watson, A. (2004) Reconfiguring the public sphere: implications for analyses of educational policy, *British Journal of Educational Studies*, 52(2), 228–48.

Z

Zone of proximal development

Zone of proximal development

The concept of the zone of proximal development (ZPD) is derived from social constructivism, specifically the work of Lev Vygotsky. Vygotsky's research was undertaken with children, not with older learners, but his theories apply equally to students in further education. The ZPD is the space or gap between what a student can do on her or his own and what that student is capable of doing if help is put in place (this help is commonly referred to as scaffolding, although this is not a concept that Vygotsky himself explored in any great depth). Vygotsky defined the ZPD as 'the distance between the actual developmental level as determined by independent problem solving and the level of potential development as determined through problem solving under adult guidance, or in collaboration with more capable peers' (Vygotsky, 1978: 86).

The ZPD is a term that is often misused, particularly in adult and continuing education. It is often, mistakenly, equated to the workshop or seminar room. In fact, a zone of proximal development is particular to each student and is a way of framing the student's past and possible future learning. The teacher's responsibility is to ascertain each student's ZPD and then construct appropriate opportunities for scaffolded support on an individual basis. If taken to its logical conclusion, this would require intensive levels of one-to-one tuition, with obvious implications for classroom practice. Vygotsky's solution to this was to put students into groups according to their current level of unsupported performance, according to one of three modes:

1. Streaming – putting students into groups according to their overall level of progress across the different curricula that they are studying.
2. Setting – putting students into different groups for each of the curricula that they are studying.

3.   Mixed groups – having students in mixed groups, and then taking smaller subgroups of students who are progressing at a similar level for separate instruction.

In contrast to the ways in which summative assessments are used in further and adult education – that is, to make judgements about a student's potential future performance based on their past individual performance – Vygotsky proposed that assessment should be carried out through giving students problems to solve that were within their ZPD, not their current level of performance. That is, the assessment would deliberately consist of items or problems that were beyond the current ability of the student. The application of the assessment would involve help from the teacher in the form of scaffolding.

Many practitioners in the lifelong learning sector have, over time, taken up the social constructivist model of teaching and learning. The notion of scaffolding and the prominent place given to individualised support that sits within the concept of the ZPD has made Vygotsky's work attractive to practitioners who hold to a liberal and/or democratic philosophy of education. The ways in which dialogue and feedback are foregrounded by Vygotsky have been assumed to remove the power imbalances that exist between teachers and students as the teacher guides the students – across their individual zones of proximal development – towards creating their own meanings and knowledge. However, such an approach rests on a partial, if not misleading, reading of Vygotsky and does not hold up to close scrutiny. Rather than promoting a 'democratic' classroom, Vygotsky, in fact, advocated a style of teaching for students over the age of 7 that would today be referred to as 'teacher led' not 'facilitative'.

References and further reading

Daniels, H. (ed.) (1996) *An Introduction to Vygotsky*. London: Routledge.

Daniels, H. (2001) *Vygotsky and Pedagogy*. London: Routledge.

Vygotsky, L.S. (1978) *Mind in Society: The Development of Higher Psychological Processes*. Cambridge, MA: Harvard University Press.

Index

A

Accreditation of prior learning, 9-10, 69, 103
Adult learning, 12, 82
  Benefits of, 21–22
  Practice of, 13
  Theory of, 16
Adult learning inspectorate, 159
Assessment, 13, 33, 58, 82
  Diagnostic, 16
  Ipsative, 17
  Formative, 17
  Summative, 17
Audit, 18, 72, 106, 151
Authenticity, 112, 125, 157
Auto-didact, 69

B

Behaviourism, 36–37
British Educational Communications and
  Technology Agency (BECTA), 47, 135
Bureaucracy, 14, 129

C

Chartered Institute of Personal
  Development (CIPD), 27
Citizenship, 56
Communication, 22, 27–28, 48, 108
Competences, 78, 112
Constructivism, 24, 31
  Social, 163
Continuing Professional Development
  (CPD), 32–33, 70, 112
Course content, 33–34, 57, 135
Cultural capital, 145
Cultural reproduction, 65
Curriculum, 57, 72, 86
  Academic and vocational, 113
  Documentation, 73
  Key skills in the, 75–76
  Personalised learning and the, 110
  Planning, 85

D

Differentiation, 37–38, 67, 73–74
Disability Discrimination Act, 41

E

Education
  Purpose of, 78, 80, 107, 149

Education Maintenance Allowance (EMA),
  104
Employability, 5, 88, 97
Environment
  Business-style, 158
  Classroom, 109, 111, 145
  Learning, 121, 125, 137
  Motivational, 94
  Political, 90, 143
Every Child Matters, 128
Experience, 17, 43, 51, 81
  Learning from, 31, 50–51, 82
  Student, 34

F

Facilitator, 51, 130, 141
Further Education National Training
  Organisation (FEnto), 2, 26

G

Gestures, in teaching, 109
Great Debate, the, 150

H

Human resource management (HRM),
  34
Humanism, 49–50, 107
Humanist pedagogy, 110, 120
Humour, 109

I

Inclusive language, 28
Inclusive practice, 39, 61, 67
Institute for Learning, 32
Internet, 47
  Use for teaching, 40, 139
Intelligence, 77, 109, 145
  Multiple, 140

J

Jargon, 4, 28, 73–74

L

Language use, 28, 73
Learners, 80–81, 120–121, 137–138
  Adult, 12–13, 158
  Diversity, 110
  Safeguarding of, 127
  With disabilities, 39

Learning,
  In communities of practice, 29–30
  Needs, 38
  Styles, 52, 83–84
  Support, 42, 129, 155
Lego, 46
Lifelong Learning UK (LLUK) 2, 26, 90
Literacy, 55, 58–59, 101

M
Memory, 24–25

N
National Vocational Qualifications (NVQs),
  93, 103, 157
Numeracy, 55, 58–59, 101

O
Observations, 99–100
  And reflection, 31
  In research, 94, 124
Ofsted, 18, 38, 99
Open University, 63, 130

P
Pedagogy, 6,7, 108
  Critical pedagogy, 19, 76
  Liberal, 86–87
  Self-esteem and, 120
  Teacher-led, 123, 137
  Theory and, 140
Policy, 4–6, 77, 134–135, 159
  Coalition, 2, 4, 5, 33, 47, 58, 70, 128,
    134–135, 149
  New Labour, 2, 4, 22, 38, 47, 59, 64, 88,
    128, 134, 149
Prisons, 100
Professional, 151
  Identity, 6–7, 43
  Knowledge, 85, 114
  Status, 59, 70, 90, 112, 142, 156
Programme review, 42, 71, 94
Psychology, 22–23, 94–95

Q
Quality assurance, 71–72, 93, 99, 118

R
Real-world
  Learning, 15, 80, 158
  Resources, 125
  Value of qualifications, 156

Recreational learning, 120
Reflective practice, 5, 92, 99, 122–123, 146,
  148
  Continuing professional development
    and, 32
  Critiques of, 123
  Experiential learning and, 51
Relevance of learning and teaching, 15, 54,
  69
Research, 11–12, 123–124, 132, 133

S
Sector Skills Councils, 135
Skills
  Core, 76
  Employability, 48, 131
  Functional, 34, 131
  Key, 75–76
  Soft, 55, 121
  Study, 131
  Transferability of, 48–9
Staff, 59
  Development, 92, 106, 112
  Part-time, 105–106
Stakeholder, 27, 61, 64, 117, 138, 148
  Student as, 152
  Theory, 152
Stereotypes, 62, 95

T
Training, 141–142
Transforming Learning Cultures, 133

U
University provision, 63–64, 71–72, 93–94
University of the Third Age, 13

V
Virtual learning environment (VLE),
  28, 139

W
Widening participation, 10, 93, 103, 154–155
  Discourses of, 117
Wolf Report, 70, 103, 116, 155–156
Workers' Educational Association (WEA),
  54, 86, 158–159

Y
Young people
  Protection, 127
  Working with, 161